MW01036680

MOUNT UP WITH Wings

A View From the Peaks

MOUNT UP WITH WINGS

A View From the Peaks

EVALINE GORE ECHOLS

Pathway
PRESS

Unless otherwise indicated, Scripture quotations are from the King James Version of the Bible.

Scripture quotations marked *NIV* are from the *Holy Bible, New International Version* ®. *NIV* ®. Copyright © 1973, 1978, 1984 by International Bible Society. Used by permission of Zondervan Publishing House. All rights reserved.

Scripture quotations marked *NASB* are from the *New American Standard Bible* ®. Copyright © The Lockman Foundation 1960, 1962, 1963, 1968, 1971, 1972, 1973, 1975, 1977. Used by permission.

Scripture quotations marked *NKJV* are from the *New King James Version*. Copyright © 1979, 1980, 1982, 1990, 1995, Thomas Nelson, Inc., Publishers.

Library of Congress Catalog Card Number: 98-068213

ISBN: 0871486040

Copyright © 1998 by Pathway Press

Cleveland, Tennessee 37311

All Rights Reserved

Printed in the United States of America

TO MY CHILDREN,

Eddie and *Sharon,*

who have provided

wings of love

under which I could run

and find shelter.

Contents

Foreword 9

Acknowledgments 13

Introduction 17

1. *Wings of Trust* (Psalm 37:3) 21

2. *Wings of Delight* (Psalm 37:4) 33

3. *Wings of Commitment* (Psalm 37:5) 49

4. *Wings of Rest* (Psalm 37:7) 61

5. *Wings of Patience* (Psalm 37:9, 34) 75

6. *Wings of Mercy* (Psalm 37:21) 87

7. *Wings of Guidance* (Psalm 37:23) 99

8. *Wings of Wisdon* (Psalm 37:30) 113

9. *Wings of Peace* (Psalm 37:37) 127

10. *Wings of Strength* (Psalm 37:39) 137

Foreword

$\mathcal{T}$he ability to find fresh insights in familiar Scriptural passages is a rare and valuable gift.

In her earlier book, *Climb Up Through Your Valleys*, Evaline Echols demonstrated such a gift. In that volume, she brought her experiences to bear on the well-worn Twenty-third Psalm, much to the pleasure of many readers.

In this new book, Evaline reflects on the familiar metaphor of the eagle as it appears in Biblical literature. God's children can "mount up with wings as eagles," the Isaiah passage promises. This word picture is the theme around which the second Echols book is written, and in it she once again brings new illumination to an old passage with skill and sensitivity.

Dr. Echols chairs the Business Department at Lee University, but she brings to her writing a much broader experience than such a career label suggests. She is the mother of two grown children, and a veteran of the daily scrapes, bruises, and dilemmas Christian parenting always includes. As an administrator and professor at a Christian university for over 40 years, she has seen thousands of developing young Christians pass through her office, her classroom, and her life. To many of them, she has been more a friend and mother-confessor than merely a professional educator, and the qualities that develop in such a process show in her writing.

Nor has Evaline Echols, in her own life, escaped the pain and uncertainty that characterizes our contemporary society. Life has forced her to learn to trust, to cope, to go to the Source — and she is candid enough to let her reader see the edges of her own need as she has "waited on the Lord."

This book is written in a simple and readable style. It is personal and accessible to ordinary men and women who, like the author, seek to know God in a direct and genuine way, without the benefit of a formal theological education. In the computer vocabulary that is so popular these days, Evaline Echols' writing might be said to be "user-friendly."

The Bible is replete with metaphors and illustrations involving animals. It was obviously God's intention to be understood by even the least sophisticated reader. He speaks of us as sheep; Christ compares Himself to a mother hen; and the Lord is spoken of as a lion. But perhaps the eagle is the example that appeals most to those of us who grew up on the topologies of Americanism.

Virtually any reader will learn much about eagles — and about God's willingness to bear us up on divine wings—from this book. It is filled with personal anecdotes, careful research, and evidence of the author's own rich and finely tuned sense of God's ability to give nurture and strength to His children.

I enjoyed each of the 10 chapters of this brief volume, and I think you will too.

—Charles Paul Conn, Ph.D.
President of Lee University

Acknowledgments

This book would not have been possible without the support and encouragement of a number of people — family members, friends, and colleagues.

First of all, I would like to thank Mrs. M.W. Brooks ("Mama Brooks" as we know her), who planted the seed for this book in a letter she wrote me in 1978 when I was recuperating from an automobile accident. In the letter she said, "Evaline, read Psalm 23 and Psalm 37." Even though Mama Brooks went home to be with the Lord in the summer of 1985, her Christian example lives on.

The motivation and inspiration I received from my parents, W.C. and Leona Gore, when I was growing up in a parsonage in Alabama is incalculable. Their example taught us (five girls and one boy) that our faith in God and His Word will stand when everything else is shifting. Now I recognize that their struggles in life were a necessary part of their development and deliverance — even unto death.

Special appreciation goes to my sister, Wanda Griffith, and her husband, Bob, who helped me to hang on at times when it seemed much easier to turn loose, or give up. Whether we were walking two miles a day, shopping, sharing books or music, praying together, playing a game of Scrabble, or just trying to get my car started, the message was always the same: "We are here for you."

My sister, Marie Carter, and her husband, Marlin, opened their home to me on weekends when I needed a haven to write about eagles. Many times, to be very frank, I felt more like a turkey. Large portions of this book were written in Gadsden, Alabama, sitting on their patio in the early morning hours.

Those telephone calls from my sister Billie Jones sounded at times more like lectures or sermons. Her prayer life and dogged determination to rise above the storms of life provided needed strength on days when the waves were raging high.

Carolyn McElroy, my youngest sister, encouraged me in the writing of this book in her own unassuming way. To watch her struggle, and then to see the beautiful butterfly of talent as a songwriter emerge from her cocoon of sorrow in the loss of our parents, provided beauty and inspiration.

To have four sisters from whom to draw love and inspiration is a rare blessing, but to have one brother (the youngest of all), especially one like W.C., provided the courage to head into the wind when the storms were on my path. Whether W.C. was calling to sing me a country song he had written "just for me" or just to say, "I love you, Sis," the message was always the same: "You can fly!"

It would be impossible to write a book such as *Mount Up With Wings* without friends. During these past 15 years I have learned that friends play an important role in this process of learning to fly. When you feel as though your nest has been destroyed and your wings are battered (or clipped) by the storms of life, friends provide that much-needed renewal of strength.

In 1981 I met such a friend, Julie Walker-Crews, when she enrolled as a student at Lee College (now Lee University). Just one year earlier, after only two years of marriage, Julie lost her husband, Paul Dana Walker, in an automobile accident. During those next few years Julie, Sharon (my daughter), and I spent many hours together — laughing, crying, praying, walking, studying the Word, and making homemade chocolate fudge when we were supposedly depressed. Julie's ability to laugh through her tears and cling to hope in the Word of God provided inspiration and hope not found in libraries.

Dr. Charles Paul Conn, president of Lee University and a personal friend for more than 30 years, is due a special thanks for taking time out of his busy schedule to read the manuscript and write the Foreword.

This book would not have been possible without

the inspirational books and poems written by such authors as Hannah Whitall Smith, Mrs. Charles Cowman, Catherine Marshall, Joyce Landorf, Charles Swindoll, Joni Eareckson Tada, Lloyd Ogilvie, and Charles W. Conn—to name a few. The devotional books of Frances Roberts have been my constant companions, second only to my Bible, during the writing of this book.

Special thanks to Dr. Bill George, editor in chief, and Dr. Dan Bowling, general director of Publications, for publishing the book. Copy editors Becky Wayne, Mark Shuler, and Esther Metaxas are to be commended for their thoroughness in refining the quotes and endnotes. The beautiful cover by graphic designer Wayne Slocumb adds the finishing touch. Also special appreciation goes to Wanda Griffith, book editor—my sister and best friend— for the many hours she spent in adding the subheadings and editing the book.

Last, but not least, the love and encouragement of my children—my son, Eddie, and his wife, Leigh Ann; and my daughter, Sharon Priest, and her husband, Benny—became an anchor of stability when the waves were high and a breeze of hope for the future when the winds of adversity blew. The inexhaustible energy of my four grandsons—Darren, Drew, Kelland, and Daniel—inspired me as only grandchildren can.

Introduction

*I*n 1980 I wrote these words in *Climb Up Through Your Valleys*:

> At times we find ourselves in circumstances where we are like a child thrown into deep water. We either swim or drown. If we are resilient enough to survive the shock of adversity, we become stronger and richer for the experience.

Experience during the past few years has been an ardent teacher. When we find ourselves in circumstances where we feel that we are drowning—emotionally, physically, or financially—if we reach up, God will throw us a raft. Many times this raft will be in the form of a promise from His Word, which will never allow us to sink, only to rise.

It was April 1, 1981 (April Fool's Day), approximately one year after writing the above words, when I found myself treading troubled waters in the sea of life. The storm had hit, and the waves of sorrow and disappointment were raging high. What do you do? Do you panic and drown? Or if someone throws you a raft, do you cling to it and hang on? The choice is yours. The choice was mine.

While treading these turbulent, emotional waters,

I felt as though I had gone under for the second time and was headed for the third. My strength was gone. But one morning in my devotions God threw me a raft. This raft was a promise from His Word: "They that wait upon the Lord shall renew their strength; they shall mount up with wings as eagles; they shall run, and not be weary; and they shall walk, and not faint" (Isaiah 40:31).

When I chose to cling to this promise, I made a decision to exchange my strength for His strength. After awhile rather than just hanging on, I took this raft for my platform—something I could stand on. The waves still raged high, maybe gaining momentum, but the Master of the sea was in control. It was time to learn an important lesson in life—the art of *waiting*.

When I realized that sometimes river and ocean currents alone move a raft to its destination, I ceased fighting the waves. Could it be possible that these waves of sorrow and disappointment are the currents designed to guide me toward my eternal destiny? Could it actually be the storm or strong wind currents that eventually guide the raft to shore?

It just could be.

Isaiah 40:31 became my platform. I read it, I sang it, I wrote it. I became convinced that this was His *rhema* for me for this particular time in my life.

The eagle became my symbol — symbolic of God's greatness, His grace, His mercy, His availability, His power, His presence, and His sovereignty.

At times I remind myself that eagles do not fly in flocks. They fly solo, trusting the high winds to actually take them to their destination. The eagle is able to ride — even to soar — the same current that drives other creatures to certain destruction.

The purpose of this book is to provide encouragement to those caught in life's storms — emotional, physical, or financial — assuring you God uses the tempests as stepping-stones (see Psalm 104:3). In the words of Jill Briscoe, "There are no winds that will blow upon me that are not the winds of His will."[1]

This book is also a reminder that difficult circumstances in your life could be by divine appointment. God could have placed you in this prearranged situation for His sovereign purpose (see Proverbs 16:9; 20:24).

Catherine Marshall summed it up when she said:

> When life hands us situations which we cannot understand, we have one of two choices: We can wallow in misery, separated from God. Or we can tell Him, "I need You and Your presence in my life more than I need understanding. . . . I trust you to give me understanding and an answer to my 'why?' if and when You choose."[2]

You and I were meant to fly. As children of God we were not made to grovel in the dirt with the chickens; we were made in the image of God, to soar in the heights with the eagles. According to Psalm 37, we can mount up on wings of

- TRUST
- DELIGHT
- COMMITMENT
- REST
- PATIENCE
- MERCY
- GUIDANCE
- WISDOM
- PEACE
- STRENGTH.

We can soar above the turbulence of life's stormy seas. We can "mount up with wings as eagles" and discover that the storm shaking our nest is the storm that teaches us to fly!

—Evaline Gore Echols

1

Wings of Trust

Trust in the Lord, and do good (Psalm 37:3).

An old seaman once said, "In fierce storms we must do one thing; there is only one way; we must put the ship in a certain position and keep her there."

So must we. At times we may see neither sun nor stars. The storm darkens our view. Some storms hit suddenly without any warning—a physical illness, a bitter disappointment, a crushing defeat; yet it is in the storms of life that God equips us for service. One writer expressed it like this:

> When God wants an oak He plants it on the moor where the storms will shake it and the rains will beat down upon it, and it is in the midnight battle with elements that the oak wins its rugged fibre and becomes the king of the forest.[1]

Pilots tell us that one of the first rules of flying is

to turn their plane toward the wind and fly against it. This lifts the plane to higher altitudes, a lesson learned from birds. If a bird is flying for pleasure, it goes with the wind. However, if the bird meets danger, it turns around and faces the wind in order to rise higher.

So must we.

One morning during the time when I was clinging to God's raft for emotional survival, He spoke to me through a devotional in *Springs in the Valley*:

> God, like the eagle, stirs our nest. Yesterday it was the place for us; today there is a new plan. He wrecks the nest, although He knows it is dear to us. . . . Let not our minds, therefore, dwell on second causes. It is His doing! Do not let us blame the thorn that pierces us.
>
> Though the destruction of the nest may . . . come at an hour when I do not expect it; though the things happen that I least antici-pate—let me guard my heart and be not for-getful of God's care, lest I miss the meaning of the wreckage of my hopes. He has *some-thing better for me*.
>
> God will not spoil our nest, and leave us without a nest, *if a nest is best for us*. His seem-ing cruelty is love.[2]

This devotional forced me to ask some serious questions:

1. How can God in His divine sovereignty use my wrecked hopes and dreams?

2. How can I accept the dissolution of a marriage of 25 years?

3. How can I be content to move from a large home to a two-bedroom apartment?

4. How can I accept the stigma of divorce as a manifestation of His love for me? (I could not accept this for a while.)

Examining the pieces of the puzzle that just don't fit only brings frustration and disillusionment. We become quite proficient in building walls of security. Sometimes it takes the removal of security to show us that these are false walls, hastily built with shallow foundations (see Ezekiel 13:14).

Leaving the Nest

Eaglets are born to fly, but the eagle must force the eaglet to leave the nest of security in order for it to learn to fly. Deuteronomy 32:11, 12 says:

> Like an eagle that stirs up its nest,
> That hovers over its young,
> He spread His wings and caught them,
> He carried them on His pinions.
> The Lord alone guided him (*NASB*).

In his book *Ask Him Anything*, Lloyd Ogilvie points out that these verses tell us three crucial things about God:

- He is a disturber
- He is a developer
- He is a deliverer.[3]

The day comes when the mother eagle stands on the edge of the nest and begins to pull out the feathers and leaves. She then takes her strong beak, snaps them in two and begins dismantling the nest. These eaglets were made to fly, but they don't know it yet. As long as these little birds stay in the nest, they will never fly. The destruction of their nest is a necessary part of their training. The mother eagle then casts them out of the nest, and they go hurling down the face of the cliff, surely to their destruction.

But not so.

The mother eagle swoops down, catches them on her back, bears them up, and puts them back into the nest. Again and again she repeats this process. What might appear at the time to be cruel and destructive treatment is actually a course in developing their unused wings of trust.

So it is with us. Sometimes God takes our lives and "casts us out" of all the securities around us. Just when we think we have our lives together just as we want them, everything seems to fall apart.

We're tempted to say, "Why would God do this to me? Does He no longer love me?"

Sure He does. More than we can comprehend.

Why does God allow the thorns in our nest to prick us and invade our comfort zones? Perhaps He is reminding us it is time to spread our wings and learn to fly. If our uncomfortable nest does not rouse us, God may allow painful circumstances to push us to the precipice. As Ogilvie reminds us, God is not only a disturber and developer, but He is also our deliverer! When circumstances force us to leap from the edge of our nest of security and comfort, we soon discover that the everlasting arms do more than catch us. They are like the wind lifting us, described in Deuteronomy 33:26, 27:

> There is none like unto the God of Jeshurun, who rideth upon the heaven in thy help, and in his excellency on the sky. The eternal God is thy refuge, and underneath are the everlasting arms: and he shall thrust out the enemy from before thee; and shall say, Destroy them.

Discovering New Heights

God sometimes uses the processes of disturbance, His brooding love, and His perfecting strength to lead us to unknown heights. It is hard to comprehend the truth that our maturity is dependent on His disturbance, deployment, and deliverance.

I once read a fable of how birds supposedly got their wings. They were created without wings; they had lovely plumage; they could sing, but they could not fly. Then God made wings and placed them in front of the birds, saying, "Come take up these burdens and bear them." At first the birds hesitated. Then they picked up the wings in their beaks and laid them on their shoulders. Although the wings were heavy and hard to bear, they folded the burdens over their hearts; then the wings grew to their bodies. Their burdens became wings.

When trouble strikes, some people buy crutches; others (like Joseph) grow wings. The life of Joseph teaches us that God's graduate school of Christian growth is seldom a one-year curriculum. It takes a world with trouble in it to train men and women for their high calling as children of God. The 13 years Joseph spent in obscurity in Egypt were not wasted years. God knew that the man who emerged in Genesis 41 had to be different from the man who submerged in chapter 37. Joseph committed his way into the Lord's hands that terrible day when he was falsely accused. He was three years under the black cloud of accusations by Potiphar's wife. But then he came forth into the light without a stain upon his soul.

The inexcusable ingratitude of the butler left Joseph in the prison where he suffered unjustly, but God was keeping him close at hand until the moment when he was needed for work of stupendous importance. While God's purposes slowly ripened in the world outside, Joseph's character developed into strength and self-discipline within the dungeon walls. He was literally mounting up with wings of trust.

Every event in Joseph's life was a part of the final result. The inhuman wickedness of his brothers in selling him, the lie of Potiphar's wife which sent him to the dungeon, the ingratitude of the butler which left him forgotten for two years in prison—all of these were parts of God's plan for his life. As the Scripture explains, "They meant it for evil, but God meant it for good" (see Genesis 50:20).

So it is in our lives.

Finding Our Security

There are times when we pray for a problem to be solved, a need to be met, or a thorn to be removed from our nest. At the same time God may be watching to see when the thorns in our nest will force us to move out and try our unused wings.

We are forced to spread our wings of trust when all worldly or earthly crutches of security are removed. The reality of trusting God comes when our entire security is really *felt* (by our emotions as well as our minds) to be in Him.

The forceful storm strikes, ejecting us from our nest of security and safety; then we stretch our wings of trust through praise and thanksgiving. What security did Daniel feel in the lion's den or Elijah in the wilderness during a famine? From the world's point of view, none.

In 2 Corinthians 12:10, Paul indicates that it is possible for us to find security in insecurity: "Therefore I take pleasure in infirmities, in reproaches, in necessities, in persecutions, in distresses for Christ's sake: for when I am weak, then am I strong."

It seems Paul is emphasizing that when we are insecure in the things of the world, we then come to understand the reality of security in the Lord.

God wants us to learn to use the winds of adversity He allows to beat upon us, not to defeat us, but to drive us to Him. "The children of men put their trust under the shadow of thy wings" (Psalm 36:7). Edith Schaeffer says:

> Could we run to hide under His wings if the noise of difficulty did not hit our ears with some kind of fearsome insecurity? . . . We need to acknowledge quietly before the Lord the fact that insecurity in earthly things can open the way to our literal running to Him and find filling us the actual emotion of security under His "feathers" in His care (Psalm 91:4).[4]

Psalm 91:15 says: "He shall call upon me, and I will answer him: I will be with him in trouble; I will deliver him, and honour him."

Waiting for His Timing

Our natural instinct is to take things into our own hands, but there are times when it is wiser to wait and be still. Those who wait on the Lord are able to transform their loneliness into times of aloneness with Him.

These times of waiting on God are necessary not only to discover our weaknesses and frailties but also to learn to commit them to Him. We must then allow Him, in His own way and in His own timing, to fill the void, to replace our weakness with His strength. He removes fear and gives faith. He strengthens the fibers of our lives to prepare us for steady climbing—always upward—never looking back and depleting our energies with regret and remorse; but as Paul said, "Pressing forward to the prize of the high calling of Jesus Christ" (see Philippians 3:14).

When we wait under the cloud of trial, we have His assurance that these clouds will burst into showers of blessings according to His perfect timing. In 2 Corinthians 4:15, 17, we are reminded: "All things are for your sakes, that the abundant grace might through the thanksgiving of many redound to the glory of God. . . . For our light affliction, which is

but for a moment, worketh for us a far more ex-
ceeding and eternal weight of glory."

One morning as I was driving to work, God impressed this thought in my mind: *Through every
wind of adversity blows a gentle breeze of grace.* When
we mount up with wings, we exchange our strength
for Christ and His strength. We can then leave our
perch of distrust, forsake our nest of safety, and soar
on wings of trust.

> When is the time to trust?
> Is it when all is calm,
> When waves the victor's palm,
> And life is one glad psalm
> Of joy and praise?
> Nay! but the time to trust
> Is when the waves beat high,
> When storm clouds fill the sky,
> And prayer is one long cry,
> O help and save!
>
> When is the time to trust?
> Is it when friends are true?
> Is it when comforts woo,
> And in all we say and do
> We must but praise?
> Nay! but the time to trust
> Is when we stand alone,
> And summer birds have flown,
> And every prop is gone,
> All else but God.

—Selected[5]

Personal Journal

In my devotions tonight I feel God is saying to me:

> I have deliberately put thorns in your nest of security to drive you forth. I understand your reluctance, but I will deal with you until you break out of your bondage.

The Lord is impressing me that it is time for me to get off my perch of distrust, out of my nest of seeming safety, and soar on wings of trust. I must admit being thrust out of the nest to try the air is scary.

2

Wings of Delight

Delight thyself also in the Lord; and he shall give thee the desires of thine heart (Psalm 37:4).

*H*ave you ever watched an eagle soar high into the sky, *delighting* in the high winds that would drive other creatures to destruction?

On wings of delight we can learn to soar above the billows of disappointment, sorrow, and suffering—even heartbreak. We can learn to rise, as the eagle, above things and circumstances. As we wait on the Lord, we discover that our strength is renewed, our breadth of view enlarged.

The higher an eagle flies, the greater the perspective of the land below. At lower elevations, the eagle is often harassed by hawks and other smaller birds. The wings of the eagle are designed for gliding in the winds, even rough winds. Normally an eagle flies at a speed of about 50 miles per hour; however, when it glides in wind currents, speeds of 80 to 100 miles per hour are not uncommon.

Again I quote from *Climb Up Through Your Valleys,* a book I wrote in 1980, at a time in my life when the dark clouds were gathering and a major emotional hurricane was in the forecast:

> There is another lesson we can learn from the eagle. As he sits on a precipice, watching dark clouds gathering overhead, he sits perfectly still looking all around. He never moves a feather until he feels the first burst of breeze. He knows then the storm has struck him. With a scream he swings his breast to the storm. It is the storm itself that he uses to soar upward into the black sky. Had it not been for the storm he might have remained in the valley. [1]

Locking Our Wings

Jamie Buckingham explains in his book *Where Eagles Soar* how the eagle "locks his wings, picks the thermal, and rides the breath of God above the storm . . . over the storm. Twenty-five, thirty thousand feet. He is now beyond his own control. He locks his wings and rides the winds of God." [2]

When we are swept beyond control by the winds of adversity, we too can lock our wings in the face of impossible odds. Nothing can hinder our upward climb. This process of losing control is referred to as "waiting on the Lord" (see Isaiah 40:31) and as "delighting ourselves in the Lord" (see Psalm 37:4). Waiting does not mean sitting idly, but it means being willing to lose control, to turn loose of our crutches and find our wings.

A few years ago I learned an important lesson about the art of waiting. While en route to Israel with the President's Council from Lee University, we were forced to wait at the London airport for three hours, delaying our arrival in Israel. Did we enjoy waiting? No. Was it for our good? Yes.

During those three hours of waiting, I watched intensely as the mechanics at Heathrow Airport worked feverishly to determine the technical difficulties. However, after the problem was discovered, our waiting would have been in vain had the mechanics not been allowed to correct it. This wait involved action. I was perfectly willing to trust the captain's orders to wait before we continued our flight to Israel. Even though my knowledge of flying is limited, and it would not have been possible for me to understand the reason for this period of waiting had the captain explained the technical difficulties, it was necessary for me to trust his judgment that at this particular time it was more advantageous for me to wait than it was for me to fly.

Checking for Difficulties

So it is in our lives. When we face these enforced times of waiting (or aloneness), perhaps our Captain

35

is checking for technical difficulties. Again, if we allow Him to discover the problem areas and then refuse to allow Him to correct the difficulties—or perhaps to strengthen an area that might later have a tendency to weaken under stress or duress—our waiting is in vain.

These times of waiting on God are necessary, not only to discover our weaknesses and frailties, but to also learn to commit them to Him, the Master Captain, and allow Him to fill the void.

Hudson Taylor, a well-known English missionary to China, made his first journey in a sailing vessel. En route, their ship was becalmed near a cannibal island and was slowly but surely drifting toward the shore. The distressed captain came to Mr. Taylor and asked him to pray to God for help. Mr. Taylor said that he would if the captain would set the sails to catch the breeze.

The captain declined, for fear that he would make himself a laughingstock to all on board by unfurling in a dead calm. But Mr. Taylor emphatically declared, "I will not undertake to pray for the vessel unless you will prepare the sails."

Finally the captain spread the sails. Mr. Taylor began to pray. While he was praying, he heard a knock on his cabin door. The captain had come to ask that he stop praying, for they already had more wind than they could well manage. When the vessel had been only a hundred yards from the fateful shore, a strong wind had struck the sails, driving the ship safely out to sea.[3]

Setting the Sails

God expects us to set the sails in our lives to catch the breeze of His Holy Spirit. This is what the psalmist meant when he said, "Delight *thyself* also in the Lord; and he shall give thee the desires of thine heart" (emphasis mine). This means setting the sails of our mind before we see any trace of the winds of achievement or deliverance—whatever the need may be.

In Ted Engstrom's book *The Pursuit of Excellence*, he quotes psychiatrist Kart Kiev of Cornell University on the importance of developing personal goals:

> In my practice as a psychiatrist, I have found that helping people to develop personal goals has proved to be the most effective way to help them to cope with problems. Observing the lives of people who have mastered adversity, I have noted that they have established goals and sought with all their effort to achieve them. From the moment they decided to concentrate all their energies on a specific objective, they began to surmount the most difficult odds.[4]

When we set our sails in one direction, we find

that the winds of adversity will not defeat us but drive us to Him. Like the eagle, we will delight in the high winds and actually use them to reach our goals in life.

Leaving the Nest

In retrospect—17 years later—I can testify that the winds of adversity forced me to leave my nest of security and develop my wings of delight. After spending 27 years in the president's office at Lee University as secretary/administrative assistant to four presidents, I made the plunge to the classroom, teaching business and chairing the department.

The five summers and one full year I spent at Louisiana State University pursuing my Ph.D. degree (which I completed in 1990 in my early 50s) were times of professional development and emotional healing. Even the two-bedroom apartment became a blessing, rather than having the responsibility of maintaining a large home while attending school.

Some of the world's greatest men and women have used their disabilities and adversities as stepping-stones:

- Cripple him, and you have a Sir Walter Scott.

- Lock him in a prison cell, and you have a John Bunyan.

- Bury him in the snows of Valley Forge, and you have a George Washington.

- Raise him in abject poverty, and you have an Abraham Lincoln.

- Strike him down with infantile paralysis, and he becomes a Franklin D. Roosevelt.

- Deafen a genius composer, and you have a Ludwig van Beethoven.[5]

And there are others:

- Put her in a concentration camp, and you have a Corrie ten Boom.

- Leave her as a widow at an early age, and you have a Catherine Marshall.

- Cripple her as a child in an automobile accident, and you see a Cheryl Pruitt Salem (Miss America 1980).

And to bring it closer to home — right here on the Lee University campus where I teach:

- Lose a husband in a tragic automobile accident in the prime of his life, and you have a Julie Walker-Crews.

- Lose her mother at an early age through cancer, and you have a Debbie Wesson Sheeks (national Teen Talent soloist winner at age 17).

This reminds me of a song we used to sing in church when I was growing up in Alabama:

God Leads Us Along

In shady green pastures, so rich and so sweet,
God leads His dear children along;
Where the water's cool flow bathes the weary
    one's feet,
God leads His dear children along.

Chorus
Some thru the waters, some thru the flood,
Some thru the fire, but all thru the blood;
Some thru great sorrow, but God gives a song,
In the night season and all the day long.

Sometimes on the mount where the sun shines so
    bright,
God leads His dear children along;
Sometimes in the valley, the darkest of night,
God leads His dear children along.

—G.A. Young

We all come to rivers in our lives, places where
there seems to be no bridge, and we wonder how
we will get across. A friend of mine once wrote,
"The eagle does not worry how he will cross the
river when the bridge is washed out." God always
provides stepping-stones to enable us to cross the
river. The mariner does not expect to see the sun
and stars every day; however, when he does, he
takes his observations and navigates for many days
by the measurements made from their light.

Preparing for Flight

The eaglet does not learn to fly when the storm hits; the mother eagle prepares it ahead of time. Today I was reading in my journal a devotional I recorded March 1, 1981 — one month before my nest of security was destroyed, when I felt that I *was* in water over my head and did not know how to swim:

> Do not wait until calamity strikes to prepare your soul. The inner fortification which you shall need must be built up in advance. . . . Men do not walk onto a battlefield and win a victory, or even survive, without preparation.
>
> No event in your life is a mistake. I will use every circumstance to enrich your ministry and perfect your soul. The opening of doors is My responsibility; but the preparation of your soul is your own responsibility. Do not fail. If you would be ready when the time comes, you must be diligent now and follow My guidance in every detail with the greatest care.[6]

Every dark cloud may become a chariot in which to ride to new heights of spiritual development. "[He] walketh upon the wings of the wind" (Psalm 104:3). When the winds of adversity blow and all our props are swept away, it may be difficult to recognize His footsteps. When the props fall, the masks come off and all the supports give way — it is then we find out who we really are. And, more importantly, who *He* is.

41

Spreading our wings of delight forces us to forsake our nest of mediocrity. Suddenly we are dissatisfied with our present level of growth; we become more excited about the future than the past. We must believe that every event which befalls us has a meaning beyond itself. Our responsibility is to ask the Lord what He is trying to say to us. His timing is perfect. Ecclesiastes 3:1-8 reminds us:

> To every thing there is a season, and a time to every purpose under the heaven: A time to be born, and a time to die; a time to plant, and a time to pluck up that which is planted; A time to kill, and a time to heal; a time to break down, and a time to build up; A time to weep, and a time to laugh; a time to mourn, and a time to dance; A time to cast away stones, and a time to gather stones together; a time to embrace, and a time to refrain from embracing; A time to get, and a time to lose; a time to keep, and a time to cast away; A time to rend, and time to sew; a time to keep silence, and a time to speak; A time to love, and a time to hate; a time of war, and a time of peace.

Experience has taught me there is no growth without struggle. We must develop our spiritual wings in His time plan. This process of development leads to complete metamorphosis. The Greek verb for "transformed" (Romans 12:2) is *metamorphoo,* which is the root of the word *metamorphosis*. The essence of the meaning is the changing of outward appearances to agree with the inner self. The way Paul found that this happens is by the "renewing of the mind."

It is said that insects with a complete metamorphosis are generally more successful in adapting themselves to the environment than others. Butterflies are among the most successful of all, having scaled wings that give them mobility and protection from their predators.

The story is told of a sixth grader who made it his hobby to collect cocoons and store them in the attic. Each day after school he made his way to the attic to observe the cocoons. One day he watched as the miracle of life unfolded. The newly formed butterfly was struggling with intense difficulty to break out of its shell and complete its metamorphosis. First it opened up a little hole; then it took hours to enlarge the hole and at last emerge through it into the world. Soon, however, the newborn butterfly fluttered its wings and flew off into the morning breeze.

The boy thought he had a bright idea. He would save the others from such a struggle. When the next one tried to emerge from its shell, he cut a large hole so it could come through quickly into the new world. Not having gone through the hours of struggle, the weakened butterfly never gained the strength to fly as it was intended to.

Teaching Our Children

As parents we find it difficult at times to push our children out of the nest and allow them to develop their unused wings. A few years ago, my son, Eddie, was going through a time of transition in his work. I was so tempted as a mother to try to protect him from some of the struggles, to refuse to allow him the pain inherent in growth. But one morning during my devotion time, God spoke to me through Frances Roberts' book *Progress of Another Pilgrim*:

> Never try to smooth out the way for either yourself or another who is passing through a trial unless you have been definitely led to do so. Your intentions may be noble, but your actions may prove a disfavor from My vantage point, because you may by your kindness thwart My work in that vessel. Always you need My guidance, even for your acts of benevolence. It is almost as hard to watch another suffer as to do so yourself, but you would find it easier if you could see My divine hand at work.[7]

In retrospect, I realize several years later that this struggle was a necessary part of Eddie's development. He was forced to develop his wings of trust—not in things, people, or circumstances, but in God.

The eagle is never content to remain in the forest.

44

Even though it is surrounded with the choicest of birds or is perched on the best pine in the forest, it will still spread its lofty wings of delight and soar upward to heights unknown.[8]

So can we.

If we face life's winds of adversity with courage, faith, and trust, we can be lifted by them to higher spiritual planes. With eagle's wings we are safe no matter which way the wind blows.

Of Wings and Men

Each winged bird was meant to fly
Over land and over sea,
Reaching upward to the sky,
Toiling upward ceaselessly.

Within the heart of every man
Are wings by which his soul can rise
To higher peaks of rarer plane
Where excellence is still the prize.

O Sincere Soul, unfold your wings
And heed the call of upward things.
Those with wings are meant to fly
Along the regions of the sky
Sunward through the burning sky.[9]

—Charles W. Conn

FROM THE PEAKS

Personal Journal

Today I am locking my wings, and I am going to ride the winds of God wherever they carry me. This is a dizzy experience, but one day I will descend at the back of the storm.

These past few years have taught me that remaining in the clouds produces stormy living. If I allow myself to remain in these dark clouds, I am convinced my life will soon reflect lightning streaks of anger, despair, and self-pity. These in turn produce rolls of thunder of physical, emotional, or spiritual sickness. With God's help I will soar above the clouds.

This week I have been reading Jamie Buckingham's book *Where Eagles Soar,* and this paragraph on page 141 was so meaningful that it has to become a part of my journal:

> Be willing for God to twist you until you are the right shape to contain your dream. God cannot put round dreams into square

containers, so He twists. Molds. Reshapes until we are prepared to hold all He has for us . . . often [He] has to do a great deal of reshaping. That sometimes causes pain, humiliation, even death. Sometimes it means we are bruised or scratched. We can choose to blame Satan when we undergo tough times if we want, but if our dream is legitimate, if it comes from God, then it is not the devil who is twisting our life but the Holy Spirit. God allows these things to come into your life for the purpose of making you a fit container for His dream. Plastic surgery is often painful, especially when it is done in public, but at the same time it is necessary if we are to reflect God's grace.[10]

3

Wings of Commitment

Commit thy way unto the Lord; trust also in him; and he shall bring it to pass (Psalm 37:5).

When we spread our wings of commitment, we yield total control of our lives and turn our relationships and responsibilities—the problems and the potentials—completely over to the Lord. Then we can soar in an atmosphere where we may hear the wind whisper and roar in the same breeze.

To commit is to turn loose of the past and reach toward the future (Philippians 3:13), to learn to hear His voice that lifts us above the swirling winds of the voices of others. As long as we are reacting to those around us, we are living in the clouds of frustration, fear, and rejection. Only when we turn our backs to the past can our hearts freely embrace the future. If we choose to hold on to our circumstances and what *we* think we need and how *we* think God should have people react to us, we will never develop our wings of commitment.

During a time of intense frustration, when I was finding it difficult to commit my circumstances to God, I was encouraged by words Frances Roberts received from the Lord:

> It is often your intolerance of your own and others' imperfections which give rise to feelings of frustration and impatience. The only way you can make any reasonable progress toward perfection is by *committing* your entire life into My hands and realizing it is I who live within you and effect whatever changes are made. When you understand this, it will be easy for you to accept all shortcomings with the confidence in your heart that as you look constantly to Me, I work within you *to bring to pass* My purposes, and I fashion you into a vessel of beauty and usefulness.[1]

Completing the Design

A few years ago I heard Barbara Johnson, who had been pricked with the needle of cancer, say that we are God's tapestry, and that when He fashions our lives, He has to put the needle in. In her words:

> God always begins at the point of our woundedness. . . . Every bit of growth we have had has been at the point of woundedness. At times we don't want God to put the needle in. We may say, "God, I

don't want to go through this." But in order to grow, we must say, "Lord, You put the needle in as You please." The more times the needle is put in, the more intricate the design. [2]

When we commit our way to God's way, we must believe God is working in our lives, even though we cannot see the completed pattern. Each stitch on a piece of embroidery is necessary to complete the design. Even the black threads enhance the beauty of the other colors. God places each stitch very carefully, even though at times this means pain. He knows exactly where and when to weave in the dark threads to increase the beauty of our lives.

At times God may be at work in our lives in ways we least expect, for the picture in our thinking and the work in which He is engaged are entirely different. "What I do thou knowest not now; but thou shalt know hereafter" (John 13:7). After we commit our way to His way, we must "trust also in him; and he shall bring it to pass" (Psalm 37:5).

The Weaver

My life is but a weaving
Between my Lord and me;
I cannot choose the colors,
He worketh steadily.

Ofttimes He weaveth sorrow
And I in foolish pride
Forget that He seeth the upper
And I, the underside.

Not till the loom is silent
And the shuttles cease to fly
Shall God unroll the canvas
And explain the reason why.

The dark threads are as needful
In the Weaver's skillful hand
As the threads of gold and silver
In the pattern He has planned.

— Author Unknown

God wants us to trust Him even when we cannot understand. "Commit thy works unto the Lord, and thy thoughts shall be established" (Proverbs 16:3). Pressure and pain are often the path to victory and understanding. He measures our trials according to our strength and His mercy.

Corrie ten Boom once said, "There comes a time when you don't walk in the light anymore. There is no light in the valley. All there is in the valley is the promise of His presence (Psalm 23:4). Neither can you walk in the light when you are abiding under the shadow (Psalm 91:1)."[3]

During some dark moments following World War II, King George said to his people:

> I said to the man who stands at the Gate of the Year: "Give me light that I may tread softly into the unknown." And he replied, "Step into the darkness, put your hand into the hand of God, and that will be better to you than a light and safer than a known way."[4]

When we commit our way to Him and also trust Him, He sends people, good music, and inspirational books to minister to us. This morning I read what Mrs. Charles Cowman wrote. She said (seemingly directly to me on this particular day):

> *Thou art not the plaything of wild chance. There is a purpose in thy life which Jesus is working out.* Let thy spirit flee for rest to Christ, and to His pierced hand which opens the book of thy life! Rest thee there! Be patient and trustful! All will work out right. Some day thou wilt understand. In the meantime, trust Him "though sun and moon fail, and the stars drop into the dark."[5]

Reaching Out to Others

This devotional reminded me of a dream I had in 1981 shortly after my daddy died (the same week my husband left). At this time in my life I

53

was being tossed about with the winds of fear, disappointment, and rejection. My inclination was to withdraw. But in the dream, which I believe was divinely inspired, Daddy said to me, "Honey, don't be afraid to reach out to others as long as you keep one hand in the nail-scarred hand."

In Corrie ten Boom's biography, Carol Carlson tells that when Corrie was recovering from heart surgery, a friend asked her how she handled the pain. Corrie said she reached up and saw the hand of Jesus with nail holes in it. Then she knew that He bore the pain upon the cross, and her pain left her.

During another difficult time in Corrie ten Boom's life, a time when she had committed her will to His will but did not understand what the Father was doing, she wrote:

> Trustingly I put my hand in His hand, like a sad child who knows his father does not make mistakes. . . . What a miracle Jesus can perform in a weak girl who seeks her strength in prayer, and what a strong guide Jesus is when even the weakest hand is laid in His strong one.[6]

God knows what He is doing. There is nothing accidental in the lives of His children. He does not work without a pattern or design. The thread of purpose is woven through every event and circumstance of our lives.

> Behind my life the Weaver stands,
> And works His wondrous will.
> I leave it in His all-wise hands,
> And trust His perfect will.
> Should mystery enshroud His plan,
> And my short sight be dim,
> I will not try the whole to scan,
> But leave each thread to Him.[7]

Just as it requires two wings to lift a bird in the air, so does it require two wings to lift a soul—a wing of commitment and a wing of trust. It takes both. Our wing of trust can become entirely disabled by the slightest doubt. Hannah Whitall Smith said it like this:

> A great many people do everything but trust. They spread the wing of surrender, and use it vigorously, and wonder why it is that they do not mount up, never dreaming that it is because all the while the wing of trust is hanging idle by their sides. It is because Christians use one wing only, that their efforts to fly are often so irregular and fruitless.
>
> Look at a bird with a broken wing trying to fly, and you will get some idea of the kind of motion all one-sided flying must make. We must use both our wings, or not try to fly at all.[8]

When we mount up on the wings of commitment and trust, we live utterly independent of circumstances on a higher plane of life—a plane no cage can imprison.

The caterpillar creeping along on the ground has a different view of the world around it than the same caterpillar will have when its wings are developed. Instead of creeping, it will soar in the air above the same places where it once crawled. When we mount up with wings, our perspective changes; we see the world through different eyes.

How do we develop these wings of commitment and trust? Isaiah 40:31 gives the formula: "They that wait upon the Lord shall renew their strength; they shall mount up with wings as eagles."

Breaking Down Walls

No walls however high, or bolts however strong, can imprison an eagle so long as there is an open way upward; and earth's power can never hold the soul in prison while the upward way is kept open and free. Our enemies may build walls around us as high as they please, but they cannot build any barrier between us and God; and if we mount up with wings, we can fly higher than any of their walls can ever reach.[9]

To develop our wings is not enough; we must

use them. The largest wings known cannot lift a
bird one inch upward unless they are used. The
power to commit and trust exists in every human
soul; it needs only to be exercised. With these two
wings we can flee to God at any moment. We must
meet our disappointments, our persecutions, our
temptations, with an active attitude of commitment
and trust. When we rise above them, they lose their
power to harm or distress us.

Singing in the Pain

It has been said that the only creature that can
sing is the creature that flies. Paul knew what it
was to use his wings when he found himself to be
"sorrowful, yet always rejoicing" (see 2 Corinthians
6:10). However, to mount up with wings is a matter of principle, not a matter of emotion. We may
experience joyous emotions, but flying is not dependent upon emotions. Flying, and eventually
soaring, demands an entire commitment and an
absolute trust. No matter how empty of emotion
we may feel, we must force ourselves to sing even
with broken wings.

> The heart that trusts forever sings,
> And feels as light as it has wings;
> A well of peace within it springs,
>   Come good or ill,
> Whate'er today or morrow bring,
>   It is His will.[10]

57

Once we commit and trust, the Lord "shall bring it to pass" (Psalm 37:5). The resurrection is proof that nothing which happens to us can defeat us. In each situation surrendered to Him, there will be His interventions and a resurrection. "Weeping may endure for a night, but joy cometh in the morning" (Psalm 30:5). Out of life's worst, God promises His best.

Only when our hearts are melted in devotion do we become pliable in His hand. "[The righteous] shall not be afraid of evil tidings: his heart is fixed, trusting in the Lord" (Psalm 112:7).

To commit means to transfer our life out of our hands into the hands of God. We exchange who we are for who we can become. The sky is the limit!

A VIEW
FROM THE PEAKS

Personal Journal

Today I have realized that I need times of quietness with God to help me rise above the swirling voices of other people. Much of my turmoil comes when I react to people. (This is where I have been today — in the clouds of confusion and turmoil.)

I believe God is teaching me a new lesson: If I can learn to relate to God, He will enable me to relate properly to others.

In my devotions, God is reminding me that I can turn my burdens into blessings or I can allow those same burdens to bury me. It is my choice.

I am learning that commitment is more than resignation. I must begin to see as Job did, that though God may wound me (or allow me to be wounded), "his hands also heal" (Job 5:18, *NIV*).

4

Wings of Rest

Rest in the Lord, and wait patiently for him (Psalm 37:7).

It is commonly thought that the eagle lives and retains its vigor to a great age and that, beyond the common lot of other birds, it molts in old age, renewing its feathers with youth.

As the eagle sheds its old feathers through molting and God replaces them with fresh ones, so must we shed our old feathers of fear, failure, frustration, and unforgiveness to make room for the new feathers of Christ's strength and new life. "[The Lord] satisfieth thy [desire] with good things; so that thy youth is renewed like the eagle's" (Psalm 103:5).

Exchanging Our Weakness for His Strength

During the molting season when the eagle sheds its feathers, it may feel greatly reduced. So may we during times of crisis; but in due season, with renovated plumage of strength, we can soar again. "And let us not be weary in well doing: for in due season we shall reap, if we faint not" (Galatians 6:9).

The key to victorious Christian living is exchanging what we are for Christ and what He is—our weakness for His strength, our ignorance for His wisdom.

When we surrender to His molting process, we discover we are no longer carrying unnecessary weights and burdens; our wings of rest are developing. We are renewed—body, mind, and spirit; we can soar above the oppressing trials and temptations. We are learning to rest and to wait.

Many times this renewal process includes a period of waiting. The original word for *wait* means to "fully trust" or "strongly hope," to believe that the things hoped for will be effected.

Twining Our Life Around the Lord

James Hastings, in *The Speaker's Bible* talks about the process of twining our life around the Lord:

> What is meant by waiting on the Lord?. . . The word which the psalmist uses signifies one thing twining itself around another and clinging there, like ivy around an oak, or like a little child with its arms thrown tightly about its mother's neck. To wait upon the Lord is to twine [one's] life, one's thought

about the Lord, [to twine one's] aspirations, one's purposes, one's emotions, and one's will . To wait on the Lord is to make the Lord the clinging place of the soul, and therefore the *resting place*, and therefore, the growing place—the place where the very stuff and substance of life is created and fashioned.[1]

When we wait, we grow. We begin to understand that God is present in the calm as much as in the storm. At times we are tempted to regard waiting periods as lost time. However, by the wisdom and discernment that we gain during enforced seasons of waiting, we fit ourselves for the possession of His best gifts. Only by waiting on the Lord do we begin to discover and understand that His ways are not necessarily our ways; they are "past finding out" (Romans 11:33; see also Isaiah 55:8; Proverbs 16:9; 20:24).

When we learn the art of waiting patiently, then we learn the art of resting in Him. Lloyd Ogilvie says it like this:

The less I focused on getting the answer to my particular question for immediate guidance, the greater clarity came as to what I should do. The Lord's will for me was to *abide, listen, wait*—to want Him more than His guidance. The Good Shepherd knew the pasture for *rest.* . . . Out of love for me, He withheld temporarily what I wanted in order to give me what I needed. . . . He sees the decisions and choices we are going to have to make. Is it not reasonable to assume that He wants to get us ready? That's His task as our shepherd.[2]

The omniscience of God enables Him to see what is best for us now and in the future. Our responsibility is to trust ourselves to His care, believing He will do only what is best for us — even if this means suffering and sorrow.

Joseph rested in Him, but he also waited patiently for Him. At the age of 17, he was sold into Egyptian slavery. Thirteen years later he was still in the dungeon; but when the time was right, God promoted him from the prison to the palace overnight. Joseph's early dreams kept him from hours of discouragement and despair. He allowed the winds of disappointment, pain, loss, and loneliness to drive him closer to God. He *rested* in Him.

Pruning

If we have qualities that fit us for a throne, nothing can keep us from it when God's time has come. We must be careful lest we steal tomorrow out of God's hands. God never gathers His fruit until it is ripe, and the fruit produced through pruning is the most precious fruit of all.

This week during a time of restlessness and fretting, these words written by Frances Roberts spoke to me:

> My child, REST in Me. Quietly settle down in My care as a bird settles in a nest. For I am watching over thee, and in love will I care for thee. There is no danger with which I am unable to cope. There is no enemy too formidable for Me to handle. I am able to carry out all My purposes, and to keep thee at the same time. Be not afraid. . . . Nothing can harm thee so long as ye are in My care, and that is forever. Ye shall be freed in Me to a place where thy spirit may soar as the eagle, and ye may make your nest in a place of safety and solitude, unmolested and undefiled by the sordidness of the world. Hold fast to My hand, and *rest* in My love. . . . My love is unaltered; I have thee in My own intensive care. My concern for thee is deeper now than when things are normal.[3]

Resting Under the Shadow

What a consolation! When we are hurting—emotionally or physically—if we will yield to His embrace, He will take us into His intensive care. His love will cover us, and we can rest under the shadow of the Almighty (see Psalm 91:1). "He shall cover us with His feathers, and under His wings shall we trust" (see v. 4). We begin to understand that whatever pressures may be crushing us have to hit God's wings before they hit us. What an umbrella of rest!

Oswald Chambers once said, "One of the greatest strains in life is the strain of *waiting on God.*" In his words, "God takes the saint like a bow which He stretches; we get to a certain point and say I cannot stand anymore; but God goes on stretching." The stretched-bow time may be a time of unbroken rest for us as we "rest in the Lord, and wait patiently for him" (Psalm 37:7).

When I cannot understand
my Father's leading,
And it seems to be
but hard and cruel fate,
Still I hear that gentle
whisper ever pleading,
God is working,
God is faithful — ONLY WAIT.

— A.B. Simpson

When we mount up with wings of rest, we receive:

- Healing for our sickness
- Power for our weakness
- Joy for our sorrow
- Hope for our despair
- Faith for our doubt.

We need not search for answers to the mysteries

of life, but trust and follow Him in the simplicity of obedience. Understanding unfolds as we rest in Him.

Venturing Out

When I rest in Him, I wait patiently and trust that God knows how much suffering I can handle. This does not imply that I will never feel pain, that life will always be a bed of roses.

Joni Eareckson Tada says it so well in her book *While We Wait*:

> Due to my condition, you'd think I would grow weary, weak, and tired of life. But because I know God and confidently look forward to the day when He will give me a new body, I am able to "mount up with wings like an eagle" even now. My expectancy gives me endurance and strength, like that of an eagle who with powerful wings is able to venture out in the mighty wind currents that whip through the canyons. . . . My body is held by the limits of this wheel-chair. But the waiting hope I have in God's future for me gives me the freedom to soar to heights of joy and explore the canyon depths of God's tender mercies.[4]

Madame Guyon, falsely accused of heresy, sorcery, and adultery, penned this poem from an underground dungeon:

A little bird I am,
Shut from the fields of air;
And in my cage I sit and sing
To Him who placed me there;
Well pleased a prisoner to be,
Because, my God, it pleases Thee.

Naught have I else to do;
I sing the whole day long;
And He whom most I love to please
Doth listen to my song;
He caught and bound my wandering wing,
But still He bends to hear me sing.

My cage confines me round;
Abroad I cannot fly;
But though my wing is closely bound,
My heart's at liberty.
My prison walls cannot control
The flight, the freedom, of my soul.

O, it is good to soar
These bolts and bars above,
To Him whose purpose I adore,
Whose providence I love;
And in Thy mighty will to find
The joy, the freedom, of the mind.

— Madame Guyon[5]

Clocking Great Speed

Right now you may be saying, "That sounds great, but what about those days when you don't feel like singing, when it is easier to identify with the sparrow than the eagle?"

Sparrows possess remarkable strength and record endurance. They appear to be impervious to severe winds; they fly continually and have been clocked at great speeds. However, as powerful as the sparrow is or appears to be, if you, a human being, were to catch a sparrow in your hand and squeeze it, you could break every bone in its body, crushing it to death within 30 seconds.

We all like to appear powerful, strong, resilient in the storms of life; but at times our spirits can be crushed and broken, our wings clipped with the winds of sorrow and heartbreak. We are left without a song.

In her book *Balcony People,* Joyce Landorf tells how stunned she was when a woman she had met casually a few times asked, "When are you going to write about the little bird?" Joyce replied, "What bird?" The woman replied quietly but distinctly: "The tiny bird who lives inside you. You know, the one that is so broken it cannot fly or sing anymore. . . . You are a strong, powerful lady. Your audiences and readers draw great hope and courage from your life's examples. You are resilient and seem undefeatable, but you hide the fact that you have been broken and that your song is gone. Someone has reached down inside of you and crushed the life out of your heart. When will you write of this? When will you admit the damage and try to sing again?"[6]

The woman who spoke to Joyce was a messenger of healing. Through Joyce's willingness to share with her readers, she too becomes a messenger of healing. Could that be part of the purpose in suffering?

Perhaps so.

Healing Brokenness

The day I read this message from the heart of Joyce Landorf, my journal reflects how I felt:

> I am reading Joyce Landorf's book, *Balcony People*, and God has spoken to my heart. In my spirit, it seems He is saying to me: "Evaline, this message from the woman is for you, as well as for Joyce. Someone has reached deep within *you* and crushed the life out of your heart. Now, when will *you* write of this? Remember, I love the sparrows just as much as the eagles. Perhaps this sparrow needs healing before it can mount up with wings as an eagle. You need not feel guilty to be a sparrow; I see every sparrow that falls, and I care.

"Today I am ready to pick this sparrow up and heal your broken heart and spirit. You must be willing to surrender your will, your mind, and your body to My will. You have been crippled emotionally long enough. I come to heal your broken wings so you can fly. I come to heal your broken heart so you can sing. I come to heal your tired and tense body so you can write and speak again."

Surrendering All

This reminded me of a message a woman I had never met gave to me about three weeks earlier at a Ladies Conference at Burnt Mountain Assembly in Jasper, Georgia.

During prayer at the end of the meeting, she came to me and said: "God has a message for you. Ever since you were a small child you have been made to feel that you cannot do certain things. God wants you to know that you can do whatever He commissions you to do."

Then she reached over and put her hand on my heart and continued: "God wants to heal your broken heart. He wants you to give Him *all* of your sorrow. Through your sorrow you will be able to minister to others if you will surrender it to Him."

Aware of the fact that the woman had never seen me before, that she had no way of knowing my life had been etched with scars of disappointment and sorrow during the past few years, I knew God loved me very much to send His messenger of healing and joy. I also recognized the importance of this weekend of rest from the freeway style of daily living.

Stepping Aside

In studying the lifestyle of Jesus, it is obvious that He deliberately planned times of rest: "Come with me by yourselves to a quiet place and get some rest" (Mark 6:31, *NIV*).

These times of stepping aside from the monotony of the everyday routine, and even service to others, are necessary for our restoration of body, mind, and spirit. It is during these seasons that we develop our wings of rest in Him.

Have you some cast-off dreams?
Some crumbled stairs?
Some shreds of song?
Some wingless prayers?

Oh, bring the bits you count
Of little worth
God salvages
The scrap of earth.

Out of your world-bent faith
And love's weak strings
He will rethread
Your outworn wings.

Till as the eagles soar
In tireless flight
So you shall mount
The glorious height!

—Mary Welch[7]

A VIEW
FROM THE PEAKS

Personal Journal

I am in Israel with the President's Council from Lee College. This spirit of Israel is contagious. Regardless of their circumstances — persecution, rejection, and so forth — they do not allow their spirit to be crushed. Neither should we. Today I thought how much we can learn from this. As Israel knows how things will turn out in the end (according to the Scriptures), so do we.

My spirit and my mind are being renewed. Being in the Holy Land is a constant reminder that the Lord's return is imminent. We do not have time for fretting or worrying about trivial matters.

We must be about the Father's business. Visiting the Upper Room was a time of spiritual commitment and renewal. Our visit to the Garden Tomb was a time of soul-searching. To stand near the place where Jesus rose from the dead was like an injection of *new life*. As I sat near the Garden Tomb, I thought of my mother and daddy who, when Christ returns, will rise first to meet Him.

Walking up and down the hills of Jerusalem today, I paused and thanked God that I can walk. In 1978, when I was lying flat on my back with a broken leg and fractured hip and could not walk for nine months, I had no idea that a few years later I would be walking the hills of Jerusalem where Jesus walked. This trip is a part of "the table He prepared for me in the presence of my enemies" (see Psalm 23:5). By "enemies" I mean rejection, hurt, and even confusion.

As we visited the Dead Sea, our tour guide reminded us that many tourists come to the Dead Sea for renewal of body and spirit. That is why I am here — to be renewed; and I believe it is happening.

Wings of Patience

Those that wait upon the Lord, they shall inherit the earth. . . . Wait on the Lord, and keep his way, and he shall exalt thee to inherit the land" (Psalm 37:9, 34).

*J*t has been said that patience can wait because it knows there is a divine clock with wings, whereas man's clock has hands. Charles H. Spurgeon once said, "When we cannot trace God's hand, we can always trust His heart."

God writes the music of our lives with design. The making of music is often a slow and painful process; the rests are as necessary as the crescendos. We must keep in mind that our times are in His hand.

When Leonardo da Vinci was painting his *Last Supper,* he was chided for standing hours before the canvas without making a stroke. He explained, "When I pause the longest, I make the most telling strokes with my brush." Patience pays.

Creating Dissatisfaction

Life has its holding patterns when there is nothing to do but wait. When this happens, it's time to develop our wings of patience. Ogilvie says:

> The purpose of the discomforting disturbance is to get the eaglets out of the nest. . . . He creates a dissatisfaction with our present level of growth and creates in us a new daring. Sometimes the preparation to get us out of the holding pattern comes with crises, and often with difficulties which force us to get in touch with where we are. There are times when God must close some doors to get us to notice the ones He has standing open for us. . . . He will use problems and conflicts to get us moving again. Whenever life falls apart in some area, He is giving us a chance to grow.[1]

Waiting Patiently

We grow and we learn—not when things come our way instantly, but when we are forced to wait and "be still" (Psalm 46:10). We want to take things into our own hands—to just do something. But there are times in our lives when it is wiser to wait and just be still. It is then we begin to hear His footsteps in the winds of adversity and to feel the gentle breeze of His grace. The psalmist said, "Wait on the Lord: be of good courage, and he shall strengthen thine heart: wait, I say, on the Lord" (27:14). "I waited patiently for the Lord; and he inclined unto me, and heard my cry" (40:1).

As the dew never falls on a stormy night, neither does the dew of His grace fall upon an impatient soul. We must have quiet hours, times of waiting upon the Lord, when we renew our strength and learn to mount up with wings of patience. Only then can we run and not be weary and can walk and not faint (Isaiah 40:31).

One writer expressed it in these words:

> Patience is character that God is building in you. It is an endurance quality. When you begin to get through your own hard times victoriously, then you will be able to help someone else.[2]

When we wait patiently on the Lord, our circumstances without may remain the same, but we experience a change of attitude within. He will do a new thing inside, while the old things outside remain unchanged.

Standing at Attention

During these periods of waiting, we must not become passive; we must be prepared for activity the moment the prohibition is removed. A good soldier stands at attention with a great deal of alertness and watchfulness, even when he is forced to wait.

So must we.

To wait is to expect, to look for with patience, even with submission. To wait on the Lord with patience is the highest form of trust in Him — in His sovereignty, in His love. Waiting is believing there is more in life than can be seen at first glance. Waiting patiently is a confession of the greatness of God. Only by waiting can we discover and understand His ways.

Acknowledging God's sovereignty is another way of saying we recognize God's purposes even in the unpleasant moments of life — the moments we would never volunteer for but which come along just the same.

One by one He took them from me
All the things I valued most;
'Til I was empty-handed,
Every glittering toy was lost.
And I walked earth's highways, grieving,
In my rags and poverty,
Until I heard His voice inviting,
"Lift those empty hands to Me!"[3]

Looking Forward

When God is sifting our lives, we must not look back and count our sorrows and heartaches. He is sifting us to make each of us a blessing.

One of Satan's tactics is to engage our thoughts

with ourselves, our sins, our worthlessness, our failures. It is difficult to plough straight ahead when we are hindered by this kind of backward pull When we look backward, our furrow goes crooked at once.

At a time in my life when I was tempted to look back, the Lord impressed this thought in my heart: *Don't waste your time looking back. You could miss the next turn in the road.*

When we develop our wings of patience, we will not be afraid to wait on God; we will have no desire to look backward. We will rise above the clouds of despair and disappointment into the realm of hope and joy. It is then we recognize that God is never late; His timing is perfect. We break the power of the past by living for the future.

Joseph knew God had a plan for his life. When he waited patiently and looked ahead, he broke the power of the past. Like Joseph, we must leave to God all that depends on Him, and think only of being faithful in all that depends on us.

Today I found a letter of encouragement (which I regard to be divinely inspired) I received from a friend in July 1981 — a time in my life when I was being tossed about in the sea of life by the waves of disappointment, rejection, loneliness, and fear of the future. This is what it said:

You have been squeezed into a narrow channel that is going to bring loneliness, but this loneliness is for a purpose — so that you might be alone with Him and with yourself. In this period of aloneness you are going to gain new resources, strength one never knew you had, and you will emerge into broad fields of opportunity and accomplishment. You are in this period right now. One of the tests is that you be alone. Learn to live alone. This is to give you an opportunity to gain insights, to look inside of yourself, and to see those that are hindered by surrounding and environmental activities.

The Lord wants you to be alone for a while with Him and for yourself. It is for a purpose. You will become a spokesperson for Him — a guide, a leader, and a strong champion for His cause. *But you have to be patient now.* How long He will allow you to be alone will be determined by how successfully you grow in your period of aloneness. He will keep you in this school of aloneness for as long as it takes for you to learn to lean upon Him and upon your inner resources. When that is accomplished and you are a completed product of His grace and His will, you will then be the refined servant of Him that He has chosen you to be.

On the wings of patience we can learn to live in a

realm where the things of earth cannot impede our progress; we can be freed in Him to a place where our spirits can soar as the eagle. The moment we set our eyes on a spiritual goal, the bondage of the past is broken. The eagle that splashes in the glory of the sun is never tempted to go back to its cage on earth.

Turning Loose

The future may seem dangerous as we turn loose of all the safety devices and crutches of the past and set our faces toward the things of the Spirit. But it is only then we learn what it means to mount up with wings as an eagle.

Joyce Landorf expressed it so well when she said you and I may never understand the reasons for the unfairness, the injustice, and the pain of life, but we can believe that God is in control and that He knows what He is doing. With this assurance we can run—no, we can soar—above the winds of uncertainty that seek to impede our progress.[4]

The soul that hears in the tumult the rustling of the Almighty Wings praises God for the storm. When we forsake our nest of false security, His everlasting arms catch us and lift us even higher.

Crises are God's pruning shears (see John 15:2). We cannot expect to bear much fruit without the pruning process. Peg Rankin described the pruning process like this:

> When a branch that has been part of someone's life is suddenly no longer there, there is pain in that life. But only for a while. Healing begins immediately, touching more sore areas every day. And the vigor that is left in the life is directed into the branches that remain. The fruit that is produced through pruning is the most precious fruit of all.[5]

We must not only think of our waiting upon God, but also of God's waiting upon us. God will not gather His fruit until it is ripe. Isaiah 30:18 says: "Therefore will the Lord wait, that he may be gracious unto you . . . blessed are all they that wait for him."

Listening and Learning

A friend of mine who was struggling with being alone and who had become quite impatient for a companion shared with me something he had read. If you are struggling with your state of singleness (or aloneness), perhaps this will encourage you as it did me:

> Everyone longs to give himself completely to someone, to have a deep soul relationship with another, to be loved thoroughly, and

82

exclusively. But God, to a Christian, says, "No, not until you are satisfied, fulfilled and content with being loved by Me alone, with giving yourself totally and unreservedly to Me, with having an intensely personal and unique relationship with Me alone, discovering that only in Me is your satisfaction to be found, only in Me will you be capable of the perfect human relationship that I have planned for you.

"You will never be united with another until you're united with Me—exclusive of anyone or anything else, exclusive of any other desires or longing. I want you to stop planning, stop wishing, and allow Me to give you the most thrilling plan existing, one that you cannot imagine. I want you to have the best. Please allow Me to bring it to you. You must keep watching Me, expecting the greatest things; keep experiencing the satisfaction that I am. Keep listening and learning the things I tell you. *You just wait.*

"Don't be anxious—don't worry. Don't look around at the things others have gotten or that I've given them. Don't look at the things you think you want. You just keep looking off and away up to Me, or you'll miss what I want to show you.

"And then, when you're ready, I'll surprise you with a love far more wonderful than any you would dream of. You see, until you are ready and until the one I have for you is ready (I am working even at this moment to have both of you ready at the same time), until you both are satisfied exclusively with Me and the life I prepared for you, you won't be able to experience the love that exemplifies your relationship with Me, and this is the perfect love.

"And dear one, I want you to have this most wonderful love. I want you to see in the flesh a picture of your relationship with Me, and to enjoy materially and concretely the everlasting union of beauty, perfection, and love that I offer you with Myself. Know that I love you utterly. I am God. Believe it and be satisfied."

— Author Unknown

A VIEW
FROM THE PEAKS

Personal Journal

This morning I am trying to draw the curtains on the past — to not allow the past to cloud my future. I have visualized a large arena with the stage behind the curtains. The space outside the curtains is larger, more expansive; it has doors which lead to other areas, and represents openness — openness to those around you, openness in mind and spirit, and openness to God and what *He* has to say.

If I try to remain behind the curtains in the corridors of the past, my view is limited, my opportunities are narrowed, and the doors are closed.

I view the first 40 years of my life, in retrospect, as the "stage era." Sure I was out front. I was in the mainstream of influence at home, at Lee College, and at church; but my scope and boundaries were limited. At times I felt as if I were in confinement, imprisoned by walls of insecurity, fear, and dependency.

All of a sudden in 1981, the curtains lifted and suddenly I was thrust from the stage (or the platform) to the large arena. True, those "stage years" influence the "arena years," but they should not limit them.

At times it is easy to long to be on stage or backstage with a full cast or family—a husband, two children still living at home, a mother and father still living, and in-laws who loved you as their own.

Yes, it is all right to remember, but the curtains have lifted. It is time to step forward to broader responsibilities and opportunities. It is time for the crutches to fall; it is time to develop wings—to soar into the future above the storm and catch a glimpse from the peaks. My nest has been dismantled, but it is for my development and growth.

6

Wings of Mercy

The righteous sheweth mercy, and giveth (Psalm 37:21).

The mercy of God moves across the trusting heart as surely as the sun moves across the heavens. God's mercy is concealed within every storm; His grace flows beneath every crosscurrent. Out of every disappointment can be gleaned some treasure.

Without mercy Calvary would have become a symbol of condemnation rather than of forgiveness. When Jesus expressed His mercy toward His enemies, He provided us an example of how we should show mercy to those who hurt us: "Blessed are the merciful: for they shall obtain mercy" (Matthew 5:7).

Lewis B. Smedes says that to forgive is to create. When we forgive we come as close as any human being can to the essentially divine act of creation. For we create a new beginning out of past pain that never had a right to exist in the first place. We create

87

healing for the future by changing a past that had no possibility in it for anything but sickness and death.[1]

According to Smedes, when we forgive, we heal the hurt we never deserved; we reverse the flow of pain that began in the past when someone hurt us. We shed our old feathers of hatred and self-pity and submit ourselves to the molting process of the Holy Spirit. Only then are we ready for new growth, for the fruit of the Spirit—love, joy, peace, patience, kindness, goodness, faithfulness, gentleness, and self-control (Galatians 5:22, 23, *NIV*).

Providing Shelter

When we mount up with wings of mercy, we provide a shelter from the storm where others may find strength, encouragement, and hope. We look through the eyes of faith with clear vision. Perhaps we cannot explain why we have been led through paths we did not select; however, we are assured that in all circumstances His mercy has not left us to ourselves.

As we climb the hills of life, with the lights behind us, at times we see only the shadows. But in retrospect we can look back and see the path illuminated with the lights of His goodness and mercy. Through the tangle of life we discover that God's ultimate purpose is to bring us into complete harmony with Him.

The psalmist cried, "Have mercy on me, O God, have mercy on me, for in you my soul takes refuge. I will take refuge in the shadow of your wings until the disaster has passed" (Psalm 57:1, *NIV*).

Under His wings—in the pains and in the joys of our lives—we may find the security of His refuge, "under whose wings [we have] come to trust" (Ruth 2:12).

> I had no hope but turning back along the path
>   I came,
> I see a gracious hand and a loving smile.
> I see a guiding light and feel a protecting
>   wing.
>   —Elizabeth[2]

Responding With Meekness

When Joseph was sold by his brothers unjustly and was put into prison for a crime he did not commit, he did not react; he responded. How did he respond? By trusting that God was in control and by leaving revenge in the hands of God. Years later, when Joseph was promoted from prisoner to prime minister in Egypt and held the power of life or death over his brothers, he refused to even the score—he showed mercy.

> And when Joseph's brethren saw that their father was dead, they said, Joseph will peradventure hate us, and will certainly requite us all the evil which we did unto him. . . .

> And Joseph said unto them, Fear not: for am
> I in the place of God? But as for you, ye
> thought evil against me; but God meant it unto
> good, to bring to pass, as it is this day, to save
> much people alive (Genesis 50:15, 19, 20).

During the past 13 years of struggle, Joseph had
been developing his wings of mercy, and the time
had come now for him to spread those wings. By
staying beneath God's wings, Joseph, as God's rep-
resentative, had now become a tower of strength to
which the fearful could run and find safety (see
Proverbs 18:10).

God prepares us through brokenness in direct
proportion to what He has planned for our lives.
Through brokenness God gives us a meek spirit.
This does not imply that we are weak; but it does
mean we are approachable, we are open to others,
and we can share our heart with others. We become more sensitive to those around us and can
detect when they are hurting.

This reminds me of an incident in my life a few
years ago. While visiting with my sister, Marie
Carter, in Gadsden, Alabama, we attended a Bap-
tist church where I had never been before. I knew
no one and no one knew me.

The usher seated me beside a very attractive
woman who looked to be around 35 years of age.
During the singing the Holy Spirit impressed me

that this woman was hurting — why, I did not know. Pretty soon she began to cry. I reached over and laid my hand on her arm very gently without saying a word, just praying silently for her. When the song ended, she turned to me and said, "I am sorry I must leave; I cannot bear the pain."

When the service ended, I went to the pastor's wife and asked who the woman was, since I wanted to send her a copy of a book I had written a few years earlier (*Climb Up Through Your Valleys*). The pastor's wife assured me that this was more than likely not my impulse but an unction from the Holy Spirit. She related the woman's story: "One week ago this morning, about this same time of day, Mary's [not her real name] husband shot himself. Not only did he die and leave her with two teenagers to support and guide, but he left everything he owned to another woman."

My heart went out to Mary; her burden became my burden. The pastor's wife gave me her name and address, and I wrote her a letter and sent her the book. This was the beginning of a series of letters and phone calls between us during these past few years.

God's Unusual Classrooms

There are times when God provides some extraordinary learning experiences in some most unusual classrooms. Do we have to learn to be human? Some people do. They find it harder to relate to people than to things. When Jesus said, "Blessed are the merciful: for they shall obtain mercy" (Matthew 5:7), He was implying something about the importance of identifying with others. However, mercy goes beyond identification. When we show mercy we are able to identify so completely with others that we actually *do* something to meet their needs.

It has been said that mercy is the ability to get right inside others' skin until we can see things with their eyes, think things with their minds, and feel things with their feelings.

A few years ago when I first began writing this book, I was sorely tested to show mercy to someone I knew was a bad influence on my daughter. This classroom experience was painful and unwelcome, to say the least. Again I realized that it is much easier to write the truth than to experience it. Who wants to show mercy in a situation like this?

I didn't.

But one morning in my devotions God spoke to me through a message on a cassette tape from the Mount Paran Church of God:

> Heed My words, My little children, for I the Lord your God call upon you this day that you will go forth into the harvest field to reconcile. . . . For I am raising you up in this

hour that you might minister to those who are in need. Accept those whose faith is weak. Accept those who struggle, and I the Lord will give to you strength that you might bear them up and that you, being strong, might bear the infirmities of the weak.[3]

Expressing His Love

On that same day, I opened Frances Roberts' book *On the High Road to Surrender*, and these words were magnified before my eyes:

Mercy is the extension of My grace. Whenever you show mercy to another, you express My love. I rejoice in forgiveness. I do not give grudgingly. . . . When you are called upon to be tolerant — to forgive — do not question and do not delay, lest you damage another soul, and your own no less.

Deal justly, but in patience and understanding, and add not evil upon evil. As I have given to you, so likewise do you to others, otherwise you violate My mercy as it would flow through you (Psalm 103:8-18; Luke 6:35-38).[4]

I felt as the psalmist must have felt when he wrote: "Horror hath taken hold upon me because of the wicked that forsake thy law. . . . The earth, O Lord, is full of thy *mercy*: teach me thy statutes" (Psalm 119:53, 64). This course in "How to Show

Mercy to Those You Dislike" was a painful experience. With God's help I passed the course. How do I know? Because today this person is a good friend.

His Word is a covert from the storms of life, and under His wings of mercy we can find peace and joy and love. "For as the heaven is high above the earth, so great is his mercy toward them that fear him" (Psalm 103:11).

In the Bible we read about the mercy seat, which was the covering of the ark (Exodus 26:34; Hebrews 9:5). The Hebrew word *kapporeth* means "covering"; the Greek word is *hilasterion,* which means "place of propitiation." The name *mercy seat* did not suggest a mere lid but denoted the act and place of atonement and the accomplished atonement.

Finding Liberty

The term *mercy seat* is therefore a happy one. The mercy seat was made of pure gold, was two and a half cubits in length, and a cubit and a half in width. On each side of it stood a cherub, with its face toward the other cherub but bent downward toward the mercy seat, and with outstretched wings, so that a wing of each extended over the mercy seat and met that of the other cherub. Between these cherubim, Jehovah's glory was manifested, and there Jehovah communed with His people (Exodus 25:17-22; 30:6; Numbers 7:89).[5]

In this fast-paced, anxiety-ridden 20th century, we still have these wings of mercy covering us (Psalm 91). We are covered with the cherubim of His goodness and mercy, which "shall follow us all the days of our lives" (see Psalm 23:6). As the popular hymn says:

> Mercy there was great, and grace was free;
> Pardon there was multiplied to me;
> There my burdened soul found liberty
> At Calvary!
> —William R. Newell

Personal Journal

In Israel

Yesterday was particularly meaningful to me. We traveled by bus through the mountains and valleys between Jerusalem and Jericho. We stopped near the Valley of the Shadow for a time of devotion. As I sat on the mountainside and watched the shepherd and the sheep "climbing up through the valleys," again the Twenty-third Psalm became alive.

Behind the sheep I saw the sheepdogs, and I was reminded so vividly of the sheepdogs of our lives that follow us — His goodness and *mercy* — that help us to keep moving forward and protect us from straying from the flock. When the sheepdogs bark, the shepherd is alerted that one of the sheep is straying from the flock or is in danger. At the time the sheep may resent these barking dogs, but at the end of the day, when the sheep are safe in the sheepfold, they are grateful.

These barking dogs in our lives are also for our safety and for our good. "Surely goodness and *mercy* shall follow me all the days of my life: and I shall dwell in the house of the Lord for ever" (Psalm 23:6).

Near Tiberias and the Sea of Galilee

Yesterday when I awoke, the Lord gave me a new thought. On our way from Jerusalem to Tiberias we were able to watch the sheep following the shepherd through the Valley of the Shadow. I noted how close together the sheep stayed. It seemed as though God spoke to me and said:

> If one of the sheep decides to stray from the flock, it is not the responsibility of the other sheep to leave the flock to find him; this is

96

the shepherd's responsibility. If one of the sheep does leave the flock trying to find another sheep, then you have two lost sheep. The responsibility of the sheep is to call on the shepherd for help. And remember, the sheepdogs—goodness and mercy—are following the flock to alert the Shepherd when a sheep strays or gets hurt.

Evaline, just follow Me, your Good Shepherd; let Me lead, and you follow. Don't try to be the Shepherd and rescue other sheep; leave that to Me. You cannot force a sheep to return to the flock; only I can do this.

I believe God is teaching me a new lesson: There are times when we need to go back and change things, but there are also times when we need to write them in the sand and allow the waves of God's *mercy* to wash over those words or deeds and eradicate them forever.

7

Wings of Guidance

The steps of a good man are ordered by the Lord: and he delighteth in his way (Psalm 37:23).

When we wait on the Lord we deliberately take spiritual inventory; we review our lives in relation to God's manifest will for us. We can then determine our position in the sea of life and find direction to reach our desired destiny. We do not deny that our lives have been storm-tossed; neither do we ignore the joys of storms past. We also recognize that in the sea of life we will be tossed around in the backwash of unpredictability; more storms will surely come.

The eagle, although fearless of the storm, does not have the ability to stop it, only to rise above it.

So can we.

Each storm has its own separate wind currents — fast, and destructive; yet we can be assured that the Master of the winds is in control. We need not fear nor be frightened but rather challenged by the winds of adversity. We can rest assured that He is ordering our steps.

Streams in the Desert gives an illustration of a man who was walking out the door in early spring when a blast of east wind, defiant and fast, blew strongly, sending a cloud of dust before it.

As he was taking the latchkey from the door, he said, half impatiently, "I wish the wind would" — he was going to say "change"; but he was checked in his spirit and never finished the sentence.

As he was on his way, the incident became a parable to him. An angel came holding out a key. He said, "My Master sends thee His love, and bids me give you this."

"What is it?" the man asked.

The angel replied, "The key of the winds," and then disappeared.

Thinking he should now be happy, the man hurried away up into the heights where the winds came from, and stood among the caves. "I will have done with the east wind at any rate, and that shall plague us no more," he cried. And calling in that friendless wind, he closed the door, and heard the echoes ringing in the hollow places. He turned the key triumphantly. "There," he said, "now we have done with that."

Then he thought, *What shall I choose in its place? The south wind is pleasant.* Then he thought of the lambs, and the young life on every hand, and the flowers that had begun to deck the hedgerows. But as he set the key within the door, it began to burn in his hand.

"What am I doing?" he cried. "Who knows what mischief I may bring about? How do I know what the fields want? Ten thousand things of ill may come of this foolish wish of mine."

Ashamed and bewildered, he prayed the Lord would send His angel again and take the key, and promised that he would never want to have it anymore.

But the Lord himself stood by him. He reached His hand to take the key; and as the man laid it down, he saw that it rested against the sacred wound-print.

The man thought, *How could I ever murmur against anything wrought by Him who bore such sacred tokens of His love.* Then the Lord took the key and hung it on His girdle.

The man asked, "Dost Thou keep the key of the winds?"

"I do, My child," He answered graciously.

As the man looked again, he saw hanging all the keys of his life. The Lord saw his look of amazement and said, "Didst thou not know, My child, that my kingdom ruleth over all?" (Psalm 103:19). "My child, the only safety is, in everything, to love and trust and praise."[1]

Unlocking the Doors

We should never complain when the winds of adversity blow. God does hold the keys, and He will unlock the right doors and lock the wrong doors as we walk with Him. The secret is to walk with Him, not to run ahead of Him nor to lag behind Him. Proverbs 16:9 says: "A man's heart deviseth his way: but the Lord directeth his steps."

Many times in our lives we think we want the keys to our lives; we think we know which winds are for our good. And God, in His love, may allow us to have the keys in order to teach us lessons. But when we begin to stray, as sheep do, into the wrong paths, His goodness and mercy gently help us to get back on the right path. He leads us "in the paths of righteousness for *his* [emphasis mine] name's sake" (Psalm 23:3). The paths of sorrow seem to put into our hands a golden key which can unlock to us treasures of truth and new understanding far more often and more fully than joy can do.

Claiming the Victory

We should never question times of disappointment,

sorrow, pain, and heartache; perhaps these represent His goodness and mercy. We can rest assured that there is no permanent loss in the lives of His children. Out of the seeds of calamity will rise a whole crop of new victories—at times in paths of unfamiliar territory. God sees the whole scroll of the ages as if it were already unrolled before Him. The future is as clear as the past. He knows the beginning and the end. Who are we to question?

The eaglet cannot learn to fly before it learns to stand. Neither can we. Before we can "mount up with wings as eagles, run and not be weary, walk and not faint," we must learn to stand (or wait). Notice the apostle Paul's admonition:

> Finally, my brethren, be strong in the Lord, and in the power of his might. Put on the whole armour of God, that ye may be able to *stand* against the wiles of the devil. For we wrestle not against flesh and blood, but against principalities, against powers, against the rulers of the darkness of this world, against spiritual wickedness in high places. Wherefore take unto you the whole armour of God, that ye may be able to withstand in the evil day, and having done all, to *stand*. *Stand* therefore, having your loins girt about with truth, and having the breastplate of righteousness; and your feet shod with the preparation of the gospel of peace; above all, taking the shield of faith, wherewith ye shall be able to quench

all the fiery darts of the wicked. And take
the helmet of salvation, and the sword of
the Spirit, which is the word of God: praying always with all prayer and supplication
in the Spirit, and watching thereunto with
all perseverance and supplication for all
saints (Ephesians 6:10-18).

When we wait on the Lord, we learn to wait and
not be anxious. While we see delay, He sees His
will being performed in ways not discernable to the
human eye. What we see as standing still, He sees
unfolding. It is like the rose that opens; the motion
is imperceptible to the human eye.

We need not struggle for the premature unfolding of the divine mystery. The revelation awaits
our arrival at a certain place in the road, and when
time brings us to that place, we shall find that however dark the "nows" were, the "afters" were worth
waiting for. During these times we learn to abide
under the shelter of His wings of guidance. We
learn to live in the here and now rather than the
there and then.

God is more pleased with our obedience than
with our understanding. We often seek to understand things that are too complex and things that
are not meant for us to know at the time.

The following poem written by a personal friend
says it so well:

I've been thinking all I can
About this life of mine,
How I turn this way and that,
How I blindly push and bind
Myself against the thorns
God has placed for my own good.
Then I think how dear His love.
It's my best He always minds
As He turns, untwists, and frees me,
Leading, healing all the time.

Moving, calling, freeing, loving
Me to come into His arms.
I'm His cherished, broken lamb-child
Lifted close within His arms.

— Rebecca Kelly Wayne

Slowing Down

According to Frances Roberts, time is as a little
wheel set within the big wheel of eternity. The little
wheel turns swiftly and shall one day cease. The
big wheel does not turn, but goes straight forward.

Time is thy responsibility. Eternity is Mine.
Ye shall move into thy place in the big wheel
when the little wheel is left behind. See that
now you redeem the time, making use of it
for the purposes of My eternal kingdom, thus
investing it with something of the quality of
the big wheel. As ye do this, thy days shall
not be part of that which turneth and dieth,

but of that which goeth straight forward. . . .
Fill thy days with light and love and testi-
mony. . . . Thou shalt experience a liberation
from the pressures of time and shalt in thine
own heart slow down the little wheel.[2]

At this time in your life you may feel that your
boat is covered with waves and God is asleep. But
remember He will "wake up" before it sinks. His
timing is perfect. He will not let you drown. He is
the Master Engineer of our circumstances when we
are willing to relinquish them into His hands. Our
trials then become stepping-stones to future blessings.

A few weeks ago I found myself in a situation
where I was trying to engineer my own circumstances. I was weary with the dark and longed for
a beam of light. Again God spoke to me in my quiet
time with Him through these words from *Streams
in the Desert:*

> Do not try to get out of a dark place, except
> in God's time and in God's way. The time of
> trouble is meant to teach you lessons that you
> sorely need.
>
> Premature deliverance may frustrate God's
> work of grace in your life. Just commit the
> whole situation to Him. Be willing to abide
> in darkness so long as you have His presence.
> Remember that it is better to walk in the dark

with God than to walk alone in the light.

Cease meddling with God's plans and will.
You touch anything of His, and you mar
the work. You may move the hands of a
clock to suit you, but you do not change
the time; so you may hurry the unfolding
of God's will, but you harm and do not help
the work. You can open a rosebud but you
spoil the flower. Leave all to Him. Hands
down.[3]

God walks upon the wings of the wind. At times
it is difficult for us to recognize His footsteps when
the winds of adversity blow and all our props are
swept away. Only then do we really comprehend
what is meant by "underneath are the everlasting
arms" (Deuteronomy 33:27). Nevertheless, He does
walk on the winds of adversity, and with Him we
can survive the storms of life. As the eagle, the high
winds only cause us to rise higher and soar longer.

Sorrows will, if we let them, "blow us to His
breast, as a strong wind might sweep a man
into some refuge from itself. . . . Take care
that you do not waste your sorrows; that you
do not let the precious gifts of disappointment, pain, loss, loneliness, ill health . . . that
come into your daily life mar you instead of
mending you. See that they send you nearer
to God, and not that they drive you farther
from Him."

Sorrows are God's winds, His contrary
winds. . . . They take human life and lift it to
higher levels.[4]

Revealing His Will

In His book *Loving God*, Charles Colson says that
it is not what we do that matters, but what a sovereign God chooses to do through us. He does not
demand our achievements; He demands our obedience. Victory comes through defeat; healing,
through brokenness; finding self, through losing
self.[5]

Hannah Whitall Smith says that there are four ways
in which God reveals His will and orders our steps:

1. Through the Scriptures

2. Through providential circumstances

3. Through the convictions of our own higher
   judgment

4. Through the inward impressions of the Holy
   Spirit on our minds.[6]

When these four harmonize, we can safely say
that God speaks and is directing our steps. Of
course, the Scriptures come first. If a "leading" is
from God, He will always open the way. John 10:4
says, "And when he putteth forth his own sheep,
he goeth before them, and the sheep follow him:
for they know his voice."

The winds of adversity lifted Joseph from the dungeon to the throne. Scripture says:

> [God] sent a man before them, even Joseph, who was sold for a servant: whose feet they hurt with fetters: he was laid in iron: until the time that his word came: the word of the Lord tried him. The king sent and loosed him; even the ruler of the people, and let him go free (Psalm 105:17-20).

Hammering Out Imperfections

Joseph was refined in the furnace of affliction as a part of God's providential plan for his life (see Genesis 37—50). He discovered that God is most in control when circumstances seem to deny it. He found that God is indeed all-knowing, all-powerful, and all-loving. The story is punctuated by the assurance, "And the Lord was with Joseph." God used the pain of tragedy and difficulty to hammer out the man He wanted him to be. Joseph had been nestled under His wings of guidance throughout his life; now the time had come for him to spread *his* wings and fly.

Leave the HOW to Jesus.
He will comfort bring;
Thru' the storm He'll hide thee
Underneath His wing.[7]

In order to develop our wings of guidance, we must focus on His footsteps. Psalm 37:23 says, "The steps of a good man are ordered by the Lord: and he delighteth in his way." The ways that others walk are not our main concern. Jesus sought to follow the Father's will every day.

So must we.

A friend of mine once reminded me: "The safest place to be is in the center of God's will."

VIEW
FROM THE PEAKS

Personal Journal

In my devotions tonight I read a story about a group of hunters who lost their way among the lakes of Ontario. A violent storm came up, and they found shelter under a great rock until the storm passed over. Then the group resumed their hunt dispiritedly until one hunter said, "Let us climb this rock; we may spy the trail from the top." It was a hard climb, but the challenge of the rock restored their courage. As they conquered the heights, they gained confidence and mastery, and the hilltop gave them a vision of the way out.

This devotional from *Springs in the Valley,* by Mrs. Charles Cowman, spoke to my heart in a special way. In 1978 the storms hit in my life, one right after another. These storms included Mother's death in March 1978, my car accident in July 1978, and then Daddy's death and the dissolution of my marriage of 25 years shortly after in May 1981. For several years I have been hiding under the rock, so to speak, trying to find shelter until the storms passed over. Now, I believe it is time for me to climb this rock. Sure, this climb will be steep and challenging, but I firmly believe that when I get to the top I will be able to find my way again. The "view from the peaks" will be clear and the trail will be visible. I am convinced this climb will give me confidence — confidence in God, in others, and in myself. When I cling to the supreme Rock, I will be above the fogs of uncertainty, fear, insecurity, and loneliness.

I believe I started this climb in 1984, when I accepted a full-time teaching and department chair position in the Business Department at Lee University and started pursuing my Ph.D. at Louisiana State University. I am not sure what path I will see when I get to the top of the rock, but I do believe the path will be visible.

It is wonderful to hide ourselves under the rock with Him, but I believe the day comes when we must climb out from under the rock, emotionally speaking, recognize that the storm has passed, and begin our ascent upward. This is what it means to "mount up with wings." We get a different view from the peaks.

8

Wings of Wisdom

The mouth of the righteous speaketh wisdom (Psalm 37:30).

*W*hen I was growing up in a parsonage in Alabama, Daddy often reminded us (five girls and one boy) that we must be "wise as serpents and harmless as doves." I later learned, or perhaps remembered, that this was a scripture (Matthew 10:16). I often wondered, *What does it mean to have wisdom?*

In the words of Charles R. Swindoll, "Wisdom is the God-given ability to see life with rare objectivity and to handle life with rare stability."[1]

Perceiving Life As It Really Is

When we mount up with wings of wisdom, we see life through the lense of perception; then we can respond with confidence rather than fear. We are reminded that God is in control—that He has yesterday's failures, today's challenges, and tomorrow's surprises in His hands. At the same time, we are able to perceive life as it really is—not the way we imagine it to be. We understand that God fashions our lives with fabrics of silk and cords of rougher materials. But we can also rest assured that His grace shines through the strands of grief and suffering.

Wisdom teaches us that when we dip into an unexpected valley or soar to the pinnacle of prosperity, we can cope with both extremes. His wisdom provides us the necessary objectivity and stability.[2]

God's gracious providence does not override human decision and action. In the story of Ruth, God used Ruth's request, Naomi's encouragement, Ruth's unthinking choice of the field, and Boaz's free decision of the time to harvest his field as instruments to fulfill God's providential care.

How do we acquire this divine wisdom? Job 28:28 says, "The fear of the Lord, that is wisdom."

Inclining Our Heart

The writer of Proverbs says:

> My son, if you will receive my sayings, and
> treasure my commandments within you,
> make your ear attentive to wisdom, incline
> your heart to understanding; for if you cry

114

for discernment, lift your voice for understanding; if you seek her as silver, and search
for her as for hidden treasures; then you will
discern the fear of the Lord, and discover the
knowledge of God (2:1-5, *NASB*).

James 1:5 reminds us: "But if any of you lacks
wisdom, let him ask of God, who gives to all men
generously and without reproach, and it will be
given to him" (*NASB*). Wisdom is something we
must seek; it does not come automatically. It begins with prayer, but it involves much more. As
Proverbs 2:4 says, it is like a treasure hunt.

In His divine wisdom and revelation, God has
entrusted to man the mysteries of His kingdom. We
should not keep these treasures stored away in hidden vaults; we should scatter them along the way
and place these jewels in the empty hands of those
we encounter. Just as the finest jewels are the most
carefully cut and polished, so it is that the hottest
fires try the most precious metal. Because Abraham
was proved to the uttermost, he became known as
the "father of the faithful."

The sovereignty of God and His wisdom is more
than our finite minds can comprehend. When we
develop our wings of wisdom, we turn loose of our
nest of human reasoning. As we draw upon His
Spirit for physical strength, we learn to draw upon
the mind of Christ for wisdom and understanding

and peace of mind. Rather than acting on impulse, we are directed by His divine intelligence.

Walking on the Waves

God has not left us to flounder in the turbulent sea of life like a rudderless ship. He is our anchor. His wisdom gives direction for our lives and also redirection when we get off course—regardless of the reason. By faith we can walk on the waves of sorrow and suffering; the storms of life will only drive us more quickly to our eternal destiny, as long as we keep looking upward. On wings of wisdom we can head into the wind with sheer delight, realizing that during times of stress and strain He reveals Himself to us in a greater measure.

Was this not true of the Hebrew children in the midst of the fiery furnace? Whom did they see? They saw the living form of Jesus accompanying them. His brilliance obliterated the sight of the flames. "When thou passest through the waters, I will be with thee; and through the rivers, they shall not overflow thee: when thou walkest through the fire, thou shalt not be burned; neither shall the flame kindle upon thee" (Isaiah 43:2).

In their storm-tossed boat, whom did the disciples see? They saw Jesus coming toward them. Had they been spared the storm, note what they would have missed.

You may be saying, "Who in his or her right mind

welcomes the storms of life?" Humanly speaking, none of us.

Frances Roberts says it so well in *Come Away My Beloved*:

> O My child, I am coming to thee walking upon the waters of the sorrows of thy life; yea, above the sounds of the storm ye shall hear My voice calling thy name.
>
> Ye are never alone. . . . Never despair, for I am watching over and caring for them. Be not anxious. What seemeth to thee to be at present a difficult situation is all part of My planning, and I am working out the details of circumstances to the end that I may bless thee and reveal Myself to thee in a new way.
>
> Ye shall live in a realm where the things of earth shall not be able to impede and obstruct and limit thy movement; but ye shall be freed in Me to a place where thy spirit may soar as the eagle, and ye may make your nest in a place of safety and solitude. . . .
>
> Seek My wisdom, and make it the guide of thy life. Let the winds blow and storms beat. Thy house shall stand.[3]

I am convinced that God, in His divine wisdom, has a hidden purpose for any storm which He allows to beat upon our lives. It is during these times that we develop our wings of wisdom. A few years ago when I was praying for a specific problem to be solved, this devotional spoke to my heart:

> In every situation, I control the forces that bear upon your life. Do not question circumstances. Look to Me for an understanding of your inner responses. Remember always that it is in the spiritual realm that I am working. Man looks upon the natural, physical world: My concern is for your spiritual life, that virtues may develop in you. While you are praying for a problem to be solved, a need to be met, a thorn to be removed from your nest, I am watching to see if any divine virtue will manifest in your responses to pressure. I am looking for true faith to express in the time of want, and I am waiting to see when the thorns in the nest will cause you to move out and try your unused wings.[4]

Witnessing His Grace

When we develop our wings of wisdom, we do not set our course by the location of other ships. We begin to understand that His Spirit broods upon the waters, even the waters of difficulty. Out of chaotic circumstances He can bring a trophy and a witness of His grace. "Where sin abounded, grace did much more abound" (Romans 5:20).

When we offer to Him our hurts, our sorrows, our failures, we find that blessings are born out of pain; triumphs rise out of the dust of defeats. During moments of crisis, we reveal our strength or weakness. The tensions of life build fortitude or expose fear.

Psalm 107:25 says: "For he commandeth, and raiseth the stormy wind, which lifteth up the waves thereof." This scripture is proof that by the time the wind blows upon us, it is His wind for us.

> God's winds do effectual work. *They shake loose from us the things that can be shaken, that those things which cannot be shaken may remain, those eternal things which belong to the Kingdom which cannot be moved.* They have their part to play in stripping us and strengthening us so that we may be the more ready for the uses of Eternal Love. Then can we refuse to welcome them?[5]

It has been said that faith may be developed in action; endurance, in the midst of storms and turmoil. Courage may come in the front line of battle. But *wisdom* and understanding and revelation unfold as dew forms on the petals of a rose — in quietness.[6]

Soaring Into the Future

On the wings of wisdom we can rise above the voices of confusion, the winds of uncertainty, and the clouds of doubt and fear. We learn to respond rather than react. At times we listen rather than speak. We look forward rather than backward. And at times, WE JUST WAIT! We are no longer content to live in the warm, soft glow of the past; we soar upward into the future with renewed determination and clearer vision. "This one thing I do, forgetting those things which are behind, and reaching forth unto those things which are before, I press toward the mark for the prize of the high calling of God in Christ Jesus" (Philippians 3:13, 14).

We may enter our valleys as pilgrims with feet, but we can come out as saints of God, equipped with wings. We are not only pilgrims of the night, but we are also the birds of God, endowed with power to mount up with wings as eagles, to respond to the upward calling—to soar in the heights.

In his book on the grasshopper, Jean Henri Fabre says:

> I do not know why the insect deprives itself of wings and remains a plodding wayfarer, when its near kinsman, on the same Alpine swards, is excellently equipped for flight. It possesses the germs of wings and wing-case, but it does not think of developing them. It persists in hopping, with no further ambition; it is satisfied to go on foot.[7]

Ted Engstrom tells a story that comes out of American Indian lore. An Indian brave found an egg that had been laid by an eagle. Since he was unable to return the egg to the eagle's nest, he put it in the nest of a prairie chicken. Knowing nothing of the addition, the hen sat on the eagle's egg, and the little eaglet was hatched alongside the prairie chickens. All his life the eagle, thinking he was a prairie chicken, did what the prairie chickens did. He scratched in the dirt for seeds and insects to eat; he clucked and cackled. He flew in a brief thrashing of wings and flurry of feathers no more than a few feet off the ground. Engstrom continues:

> Years passed. And the changeling eagle grew very old. One day, he saw a magnificent bird far above him in the cloudless sky. Hanging with graceful majesty on the powerful wind currents, it soared with scarcely a beat of its strong golden wings.
>
> "What a beautiful bird!" said the . . . eagle to his neighbor. "What is it?"
>
> "That's an eagle—the chief of the birds," the neighbor clucked. "But don't give it a second thought. You could never be like him."
>
> So the changeling eagle never gave it another thought. And it died thinking it was a prairie chicken.[8]

Shaking Our Nest

Through divine wisdom we become what God intended us to be from the beginning. We shake our nest of mediocrity and soar toward the peaks of excellence. Developing our wings is not always easy. Wisdom forces us to shake off the prairie-chicken mentality and reprogram ourselves to the eagle lifestyle — the plan God had for our life in the first place.

A VIEW FROM THE PEAKS

Personal Journal

The March wind is whistling outside, and I am finding it difficult to go to sleep again. I pray for rest tonight.

In my devotions tonight it seems that God is reminding me that my times are governed by His wisdom. Just as pieces of a jigsaw puzzle fit but one way, so does He work out the details of my life in His own time, not mine.

This is my prayer for tonight:

> Father, I pray that You will strengthen my wings of wisdom. Help me to turn my weaknesses into strengths; help me to rise above the mundane and reach for excellence.

Clothe me with strength; endow me with
Your peace. Fasten me to the Rock who will
be my anchor, no matter how fierce the
· storms. Teach me the art of waiting on You.
Help me to delight myself in You and to have
faith to believe that You will give me the
desires of my heart. Lord, help me to remember that "a man's heart deviseth his way: but
the Lord directeth his steps" (Proverbs 16:9).
Help me to follow You one step at a time.
Please don't turn loose of my hand.

This morning I awoke around 3:30 a.m. Until
5:30 I read one of Catherine Marshall's books, *A
Closer Walk*. This book includes excerpts from her
personal journal, and parts of it really spoke to my
heart. She also shared dreams she had and things
God had taught her through her dreams.

When I finally went to sleep around 5:30 a.m., I
had a strange dream.

I dreamed I was flying from Birmingham, Alabama, to Memphis, Tennessee; and when the small
commuter plane I was on took off, I could see no
pilot on board.

I soon realized the plane had been programmed
ahead of time as to when to land and when to take
off. During the first part of the flight, I was totally
alone. At other times when the plane would land,
others joined me on the flight. But we had to trust

that whoever programmed the flight instructions knew when we should land and when we should take off again.

I prayed for God to help me learn a lesson through this dream. Seemingly He is saying to me:

> I am in control of your life. Before you were born I charted your flight schedule on earth. At times *you will be totally alone.* At other times on this earthly flight, there will be those who will be flying along with you. Remember, this is *My decision,* not yours.

> You must learn to trust Me and not be afraid. Sure, we will encounter some turbulence at times. That is when you must buckle your spiritual seat belt, cling to My Word, and hold on. Do not be afraid; *I am in control.* Remember no storm can last forever.

> Take advantage of these times of aloneness. Get to know Me better. I will *never* leave you nor forsake you, but I will go with you all the way, even unto the end of the world.

This dream has been an encouragement to me. Again I am reminded that God, in His divine wisdom, knows what He is doing. My responsibility is to follow Him.

9

Wings of Peace

Mark the perfect man, and behold the upright: for the end of that man is peace (Psalm 37:37).

*O*n the wings of peace we can cross the bridge from the past to the present and can face the future with faith and courage—unafraid. A devotional which I recorded in my personal journal on February 12, 1986, says it so well:

> My child, you have crossed a bridge. Reach not back. Move ahead and press into the fullness of all I have prepared for you. It is the blossoming of that which long ago was planted and for many years has been nurtured. It is waiting for you to step forward and receive. Do not tarry, and do not question, neither allow doubts to enter your mind. Your heart may cry out and rebel, but if you will turn to Me in those moments, I will give you *my peace*.[1]

We find peace when we rest in the shadow of His

hand. This resting place is in the center of His will, which disregards outward circumstances and emotions. When we discover who He is through study of His Word and learn to communicate with Him though praise and worship, we have no need to seek peace. *He is our peace.* "Great peace have those who love Your law" (Psalm 119:165, *NKJV*). "The Lord will give strength unto his people; the Lord will bless his people with peace" (Psalm 29:11). "Thou wilt keep him in perfect peace, whose mind is stayed on thee: because he trusteth in thee" (Isaiah 26:3). When this happens, we automatically reduce our activities and dispose of nonessentials.

Utilizing the Currents

It has been said that while other birds sit and chatter among themselves, the eagle flies alone. He must, without exception, pursue what is instinctively in his heart. It is during these times that the eagle becomes a master of the wind, utilizing currents not available at lower altitudes.[2]

So can we.

When we mount up with wings of peace, we pursue solitude, not as an escape but to be alone with God. It is then that He can pick up the broken pieces of our heart and make it like new. He can gather our tears, for they are precious to Him (Psalm 56:8).

Of this process of giving Him our broken hearts, Frances Roberts said:

> Make it as tangible a transaction as possible, and visualize your own hand laying the physical organ of your heart in His hands. Say to Him, "Take this, Loving Master and Wonderful Lord, and do with it as pleases Thee." [3]

The day I read this, my journal reflected my prayer of surrender:

> Father, I give You *my* heart. Please heal it and make it like new. Lord, fill my heart with Your love so that I will have the capacity to love others. Lord, remove any trace of bitterness, any roots of distrust, any spot of suspicion or self-pity, anything that blocks my communication with You and with others.

When we emerge from our cocoons of self-pity and fear on the wings of peace, our tears and hurts from yesteryear will be mere memories. We will recognize that we are encased in the cocoon of His love. And in His appointed time He will use something or someone to open the door, and we will emerge on wings of peace. We will be able then to substitute peace for pressure and a positive attitude for a negative attitude. As the apostle Paul said, we possess a "peace . . . which surpasses all understanding" (Philippians 4:7, *NKJV*).

Focusing on Challenges

In the winds of adversity we move to higher altitudes; He lifts the gloom and removes the stinging pain of depression. We leave the ranks of worm-grubbing prairie chickens and soar in the heights with the eagles. We refuse to brood over what is gone; we focus on the present challenges which require our undivided attention.

Job is an example of one who handled a series of grief-laden ordeals with peace. How?

1. He looked up—he claimed God's sovereignty (Job 1:21, 22).

2. He looked ahead—he endured today by envisioning tomorrow (19:25-27).

3. He looked within—he confessed his inability to put the pieces of the puzzle of his life together (42:2-4).

Hannah Hurnard says that real bitterness and unbearable pain in sorrow and loss lie in trying to hold on to the things we can no longer keep, in the refusal to let go willingly, in the desperate and frantic clinging to the objects which we treasure, the idols of our hearts.[4] We must turn loose; we must let go.

Amy Carmichael reminds us that peace lies in acceptance and the willingness to let go. It has been

128

said that everything that is willingly laid down for
love's sake bears in it the germ of resurrection life
(Matthew 22:36-39; James 2:8).

Watching the Waves

Jesus walks the stormy seas of life today, just as
He walked the waves of Galilee. When we stretch
our wings of peace, we leave our little boat and
walk the waves toward Him. Peter was doing the
safest thing when he got out of his storm-tossed boat
at Jesus' invitation. Yet Peter watched the waves
when he should have been walking them.

And so do we.

Each wave in the stormy seas of life is a step toward Him if we make it so. The choice is ours: Will
we watch the waves or walk them?

This reminds me of a song we sing quite often
which says:

Peace in the Midst of the Storm

When the world that I've been living in collapses
at my feet,
When my life is shattered and torn;
When I'm windswept and battered I cling to His
hand
And find peace in the midst of the storm.

Chorus

There is peace in the midst of my storm-tossed sea;
There's an anchor, there's a rock, to build my
faith upon.
Jesus rides in my vessel, so I'll fear no alarm;
He gives me peace in the midst of the storm.

—Stephen R. Adams

Copyright 1978 Pilot Point Music (Admin. by the Copyright Company, Nashville, TN). All rights reserved. International Copyright secured. Used by permission.

When we mount up with wings of peace, we learn to be at peace with ourselves. In her book *The Gift From the Sea*, Anne Morrow Lindbergh says: "I want first of all . . . to be at peace with myself. I am seeking perhaps what Socrates asked for . . . when he said, 'May the outward and inward man be one.' "[5]

Gordon MacDonald refers to being at peace with one's self as bringing "order to your private world." He says the private world can be divided into five sectors:

1. Motivation—are we driven or called people?

2. Time management—what do we do and how do we allocate our time?

3. Intellectual—what are we doing with our minds?

4. Spiritual—what about our communion with God?

5. Rest—are we at peace with God, ourselves, and others?[6]

During a series of crises in my life, I again received a letter from a friend which helped me to face the broken pieces of my fractured life and seek to know His unbreakable peace. These are excerpts from the letter:

> You have been hit with many hammer blows lately, any one of which could have paralyzed your feelings—your mother's death, the car accident, the dissolution of your marriage of 25 years, and then the death of your father. But what has happened becomes a part of your treasury of experiences. As you come to the neck of the tunnel, there will be someone waiting there for you, and you will not be on the plateau alone. But the vale will cause you to almost forget the plateau from which you emerged. The plateau where you will end will be so broad, with such fertile plains, that you will be above the valley. Remember—no one could ever climb Matterhorn except through the crevice.

Tunneling Through

So it is in our lives. When we cannot go through the valley or soar over the mountain, God provides a tunnel of peace through which we can crawl. This tunnel may be narrow and dark and we may feel alone for sure, but we can rest assured that there *is* light at the end of the tunnel. We can know too that a tunnel is never on a siding—it is planned to lead somewhere.

Lessons we learn through our tunnel experiences are gifts from God; it is here that we get to know the Prince of Peace in a more intimate way. "Peace I leave with you, my peace I give unto you: not as the world giveth, give I unto you" (John 14:27).

Later when I read this poem in my devotions, God confirmed to me that the letter from my friend was divinely inspired:

Though the tunnel may be tedious through
    the narrow, darkened way,
Yet it amply serves its purpose—soon it brings
    the light of day:
And the way so greatly dreaded, as we backward
    take a glance,
Shows the skill of careful planning: never the
    result of chance!

Is your present path a tunnel, does the darkness
    bring you fear?
To the upright, oh, remember, He doth cause
    a light to cheer.
Press on bravely, resting calmly, though a way
    you dimly see,
Till, at length, so safely guided, you emerge
    triumphantly.

—Selected[7]

FROM THE PEAKS

Personal Journal

This morning I have been preparing to teach Sunday school, and my topic is "Fold Your Tent in the Wilderness for the Last Time." My text is Joshua 3. In my spirit, I believe God is saying to me:

> My child, it is time for you to fold your tent for the last time in the wilderness of fear and loneliness. Follow Me closely. When My presence directs you to move, go forward. When My presence directs you to be still, wait on Me. Do not move ahead unless My presence goes before you. Know that I am your guide and your shepherd of peace. I go before you and My goodness and mercy follow you.
>
> There are unexplored territories to be discovered in your life. Remember when the floods come, I will give you the courage to step into

the water with full assurance that I will part the waters or that I will walk through the waters with you.

You are My child, and I love you. Be at peace. Don't be content to remain in the wilderness. Canaan is just ahead.

Trust *Me*!

10

Wings of Strength

The salvation of the righteous is of the Lord: he is their strength in the time of trouble (Psalm 37:39).

*W*hat do you think of when you see an eagle soaring through the sky? Freedom and strength—dependability of flight. Because of its strength, the eagle has been a symbol of war and imperial power since Babylonian times. John Keats imagined the Spanish explorer Cortez staring "with eagle eyes" at the Pacific. Charles Lindberg, who in 1927 became the first man to fly the Atlantic alone, was known as the "Lone Eagle."

In 1982, we celebrated the 200th anniversary of the bald eagle as the centerpiece in the seal of the United States; this was the "Year of the Eagle."

Why is the eagle referred to as "king of birds"? Ezekiel 1:10 says that the four living creatures "also had the face of an eagle." In Revelation 4:7, the eagle is used as a symbol of strength: "And the fourth beast was like a flying eagle."

Gaining Strength

The eagle, more than any other bird, portrays the attributes of God by his strength, beauty, solemnity, majesty, fearlessness, and freedom. "Ye have seen what I did unto the Egyptians, and how I bare you on eagles' wings, and brought you unto myself" (Exodus 19:4). We were created in the image of God; therefore, we too have many things in common with the eagle.

How do we develop our wings of strength? Joseph gained strength by his purity. The story of his temptation, which led to his imprisonment, proved his fidelity to his master and his loyalty to God. It was a part of his development which made him the stable, self-reliant, *strong* man that he became. Joseph's purity allowed him to read God's will in the dreams of the butler, the baker, and the king. Tennyson said, "My strength is as the strength of ten, because my heart is pure."[1]

Isaiah 40:31 says, "They that wait upon the Lord shall *renew their strength*." The word *renew* means to put a new thing in place of an old thing. This condition of waiting on the Lord must be met before we can expect the renewal of our strength. In order to develop strong muscular arms, these arms must be used to render hard and constant service. So must our spiritual muscles. This exercise of waiting may also prove to be the means whereby our strength is renewed. With this renewed strength, we can soar, we can run, we can walk.

Augustine once said: "O Lord our God, under the shadow of Your wings let us hope, and You protect us and carry us. . . . When You are our strength, it is real strength; but when it is our own strength, it is nothing but weakness."[2]

In the words of J.H. Jowett: "Let us sing even when we do not feel like it, for thus we may give wings to leaden feet and turn weariness into *strength*"[3] (see Acts 16:25).

Preening Our Lives

Because the wings and feathers are the eagle's primary means of obtaining food, each morning the eagle spends at least an hour preening his feathers. Preening is a process in which each feather is passed through the beak simultaneously with exhaled air. This also seals the individual hairs of the feathers together much like a zip lock. Through the course of the day these feathers will be beaten and will take much abuse from the wind.

How can we relate the preening process to our lives? The mind is the battlefield in spiritual warfare. If we develop the habit of spending at least an hour each morning preening each thought through the beak of the Holy Spirit and the Word of God, this will seal our minds to prepare us to face the winds of abuse and negativism—which are sure to blow. "Be renewed in the spirit of your mind" (Ephesians 4:23). Experiences during these past 17 years have taught me that unexpectedly the waters in life may be tossed into a storm.

We cannot escape the crisis experiences if we desire to grow and mature; neither should we fear them, for His grace and His equanimity shall be as a strong anchor to hold us fast and we shall not be driven off course. Each crisis is but a wave on the same sea. In each of them, there is a purpose. It is during these times that we develop our wings of strength. When we stretch our spiritual wings, we discover that life has gained new powers, extraordinary capacity, and added *strength*. God measures our trials according to *our* strength and *His* mercy. Philippians 4:13 says, "I can do all things through Christ which strengtheneth me."

The eagle mounts up with remarkable rapidity and is noted for its swiftness of flight (Exodus 19:4; 2 Samuel 1:23; Job 39:27; Proverbs 23:5). The winged life is characterized by four things:

- Buoyancy
- Loftiness
- Comprehensiveness
- Proportion

When the eagle soars above the storm, it sees the earth from a different perspective. So can we. When we rise above the thundering voices of confusion, the dark clouds of doubt and fear, and the fog of human weakness on the wings of strength, we see life from a different perspective. We recognize that God uses the things that weaken us to strengthen us. Our viewpoint of others — even our enemies — changes because we see things from God's point of view. The things that worry us lose their grip; the things that weaken us, God turns into strength. "For my strength is made perfect in weakness" (2 Corinthians 12:9). "And as thy days, so shall thy strength be" (Deuteronomy 33:25).

Charles Swindoll says that heartaches and disappointments are like the hammer, the file, and the furnace. In his words: "They come in all shapes and sizes . . . a broken home or marriage. . . . Do I write to a 'nail' that has begun to resent the blows of the hammer? Are you at the brink of despair, thinking you cannot bear another day of heartache?"[4]

As difficult as it may be for you to believe this day, the Master knows what He's doing. Your Savior knows your breaking point.

Like David when calamity caved in, *strengthen yourself in the Lord your God* (see 1 Samuel 30:6). God's hand is in your heartache. Swindoll reiterates that those whom God uses most effectively have been hammered, filed, and tempered in the furnace of trials and heartaches.[5]

Purifying

Proverbs 24:10 says: "If thou faint in the day of adversity, thy strength is small." But in verse 5 we read, "A wise man is strong; yea, a man of knowledge increaseth *strength.*"

When the bottom drops out, God is building, strengthening, and purifying us. He will never destroy us through adversity; His purpose is to strengthen and build character.

When we wait on the Lord, in faith, we develop wings of strength to rise above the mundane, we have stamina for endurance, and we find grace for dogged persistence. When the pain of waiting robs us of the power to believe, we learn to trust. In Psalm 37 we find words of encouragement and strength which focus on the Lord—not on self, and not on others:

- "Trust in *the Lord*, and do good" (v. 3).

- "Wait for *the Lord* and keep his way" (v. 34, *NIV*).

- "The salvation of the righteous comes from *the Lord*; he is their stronghold in time of trouble" (v. 39, *NIV*).

Drawing Strength From His Resources

At times we may find ourselves waiting on others to supply our strength. On the other hand, we must also be aware that others may literally drain us of strength by their actions, deeds, or maybe just their indifference. But Isaiah 40:31 says, "They that wait upon *the Lord* shall renew their strength."

This has been a difficult lesson for me to learn. It is so easy to depend on family and friends for strength and encouragement. But God wants to teach us to wait on Him, to draw from His resources through the Word and through communion with Him in prayer and praise. When we talk to Him, we shift the focus from ourselves to Him and to those around us who are hurting. Perhaps the dark clouds are still gathering, but when we look *to Him*, we begin to see the clear forecast of the dawn. On the wings of strength, we rise above the fogs of adversity and the mists of doubt and fear.

My journal reflects a devotional from Frances Roberts which was especially meaningful to me at a time when I was trying desperately to find comfort and strength from those around me:

O My little one, take courage; let your heart be strong, for I am near. I am your strong support. I will not allow your foot to slip, I will give you security and comfort, and you will know that it is from My hand it has come.

Look not about for love to come to you; look rather to see where you may give it. Do not tarry for convenience nor opportunity. Give a sacrificial portion. Make the out-of-season gesture of kindness.[6]

It is amazing the inner strength we discover when we shift our focus from ourselves to those around us—not reaching to them to provide crutches for us, but providing wings of strength for them whereby they may run and find safety from the storm.

A VIEW FROM THE PEAKS

Personal Journal

Tonight God is reminding me through His Word that He is my stronghold in time of trouble. Psalm 73:26 says: "My flesh and my heart may fail, but God is the strength of my heart and my portion forever" (*NIV*).

I have just read Larry Richards' book titled *When It Hurts Too Much to Wait*, and these words spoke to me:

Our relationship with God is like a fortress. When troubles come, we hurry to Him, and behind the massive walls and shuttered windows of *His strength* we know security. We wait for the Lord. But we also wait in the Lord. . . .

Without the waiting, yesterday's pain would never have given birth to today's joy.[7]

I feel tired in body this morning and a little weary in spirit. It seems God is saying to me:

I have brought you to this place in the road of life. My desire is to make you *strong.* Drink in the silence. Listen to the silence; it will build strength. My plans and purposes reach far beyond your present view. You have climbed up through your valleys; now take a look from the mountain peaks!

143

Notes

Introduction

[1]Jill Briscoe, *Wings* (Nashville: Thomas Nelson Publishers, 1984) January 2.

[2]Catherine Marshall, *Meeting God at Every Turn* (Carmel, NY: Guideposts, 1980) 231, 251.

Chapter 1

[1]Mrs. Charles Cowman, *Streams in the Desert*, vol. 1 (Grand Rapids: Zondervan Publishing House, 1925) 18.

[2]Mrs. Charles Cowman, *Springs in the Valley* (Grand Rapids: Zondervan Publishing House, 1939) 136.

[3]Lloyd J. Ogilvie, *Ask Him Anything* (Carmel, NY: Guideposts, 1981) 237.

[4]Edith Schaeffer, *A Way of Seeing* (Old Tappan, NJ: Fleming H. Revell Co., 1977) 86.

[5]Cowman, *Streams*, vol. 1, 215-16.

Chapter 2

[1]Evaline Echols, *Climb Up Through Your Valleys* (Cleveland, TN: Pathway Press, 1980) 134.

[2]Jamie Buckingham, *Where Eagles Soar* (Lincoln, VA: Chosen Books, 1980) 13-14.

[3]George E. Failing, ed., *With Open Face* (Marion, IN: The Wesley Press, 1983) 13.

[4]Ted W. Engstrom, *The Pursuit of Excellence* (Grand

145

Rapids: Zondervan Publishing House, 1982) 26.

[5]Engstrom, *Pursuit* 82.

[6]Frances J. Roberts, *Progress of Another Pilgrim* (Ojai, CA: The King's Press, 1970) 22.

[7]Roberts, *Progress* 88.

[8]Mrs. Charles Cowman, *Streams in the Desert,* vol. 1 (Grand Rapids: Zondervan Publishing House, 1925) 251.

[9]Charles W. Conn, "Of Wings and Men," *The Lighted Pathway,* Sept. 1983: cover.

[10]Buckingham, *Eagles Soar* 141.

Chapter 3
[1]Frances J. Roberts, *Progress of Another Pilgrim* (Ojai, CA: The King's Press, 1970) 84.

[2]Barbara Johnson, "The Creativity of God," audiocassette, rec., Dalton, GA, n.d.

[3]Carole C. Carlson, *Corrie ten Boom: Her Life, Her Faith: A Biography* (Old Tappan, NJ: Fleming H. Revell Co., 1983) 54, 100.

[4]George Shinn, *The Miracle of Motivation* (Wheaton, IL: Tyndale House, 1981) 197.

[5]Mrs. Charles Cowman, *Springs in the Valley* (Grand Rapids: Zondervan Publishing House, 1939) 276.

[6]Carlson, *Corrie* 54, 100.

[7]Paul E. Billheimer, *Don't Waste Your Sorrows* (Fort

Washington, PA: Christian Literature Crusade, 1977) 107.

[8]Hannah Whitall Smith, *The Christian's Secret to a Happy Life* (Old Tappan, NJ: Fleming H. Revell Co., 1952) 244.

[9]Smith, *Christian's Secret* 245.

[10]Smith, *Christian's Secret* 248.

Chapter 4
[1]James Hastings, *The Speaker's Bible*, vol. 3, *Psalms II* (Grand Rapids: Baker Book House, 1978) 192.

[2]Lloyd J. Ogilvie, *God's Will for Our Lives* (Eugene, OR: Harvest House Publishers, 1982) 35-36.

[3]Frances J. Roberts, *Come Away My Beloved* (Old Tappan, NJ: Fleming H. Revell Co., 1973) 91.

[4]Joni Eareckson Tada, *While We Wait* (Grand Rapids: Zondervan Publishing House, 1982) 12.

[5]Kay Arthur, *His Imprint, My Expression: Changed Forever by the Master's Touch* (Eugene, OR: Harvest House Publishers, 1993) 44-45.

[6]Joyce Landorf, *Balcony People* (Waco, TX: Word Books, 1984) 19-20.

[7]Mary Welch, *More Than Sparrows* (Grand Rapids: Zondervan Publishing House, 1976) 16.

Chapter 5
[1]Lloyd J. Ogilvie, *Ask Him Anything* (Carmel, NY:

Guideposts, 1981) 235, 237, 238.

²Barbara Lee Johnson, *Count It All Joy* (Grand Rapids: Baker Book House, 1976) 23.

³Charles R. Swindoll, *Improving Your Serve* (Waco, TX: Word Books, 1981) 190.

⁴Joyce Landorf, *Irregular People* (Waco, TX: Word Publishers, 1982) 134-35.

⁵Peg Rankin, *Yet Will I Trust Him* (Ventura, CA: Regal Books, 1980) 89.

Chapter 6
¹Lewis B. Smedes, *Forgive and Forget* (San Francisco: Harper and Row Publishers, 1984) 152.

²David Atkinson, *Wings of Refuge* (Downers Grove, IL: InterVarsity Press, 1983) 29.

³Sermon, rec., Mount Paran Church of God, Atlanta, GA, 1983.

⁴Frances J. Roberts, *On the High Road to Surrender* (Ojai, CA: King's Farspan, Inc., 1973) 50.

⁵John D. Davis and Henry Snyder Gehmun, eds., *The Westminster Dictionary of the Bible* (Philadelphia: The Westminster Press, 1944) 390-91.

Chapter 7
¹Mrs. Charles Cowman, *Streams in the Desert*, vol. 1 (Grand Rapids: Zondervan Publishing House, 1925) 134-35.

[2]Frances J. Roberts, *Come Away My Beloved* (Old Tappan, NJ: Fleming H. Revell Co., 1973) 30-31.

[3]Cowman, *Streams*, vol. 1, 100.

[4]Mrs. Charles Cowman, *Streams in the Desert*, vol. 2 (Grand Rapids: Zondervan Publishing House, 1966) February 26.

[5]Charles Colson, *Loving God* (Grand Rapids: Zondervan Publishing Co., 1983) 25.

[6]Hannah Whitall Smith, *The Christian's Secret to a Happy Life* (Old Tappan, NJ: Fleming H. Revell Co., 1952) 136.

[7]Mrs. Charles Cowman, *Springs in the Valley* (Grand Rapids: Zondervan Publishing House, 1939) 139.

Chapter 8
[1]Charles R. Swindoll, *Living on the Ragged Edge* (Waco, TX: Word Books, 1985) 208.

[2]Swindoll, *Living* 208.

[3]Frances J. Roberts, *Come Away My Beloved* (Old Tappan, NJ: Fleming H. Revell Co., 1973) 13, 46, 52.

[4]Frances J. Roberts, *Progress of Another Pilgrim* (Ojai, CA: The King's Press, 1970) 86.

[5]Mrs. Charles Cowman, *Springs in the Valley* (Grand Rapids: Zondervan Publishing House, 1939) 287.

[6]Roberts, *Progress* 28.

[7]Jean Henri Fabre, *The Life of the Grasshopper*, trans. Alexander Texera de Mattos (New York: Dodd, Mead and Co., 1920) 374-75.

[8]Ted W. Engstrom, *The Pursuit of Excellence* (Grand Rapids: Zondervan Publishing House, 1982) 15-16.

Chapter 9
[1]Frances J. Roberts, *On the High Road to Surrender* (Ojai, CA: King's Farspan, Inc., 1973) 55.

[2]Kenneth L. Price, *The Eagle Christian* (Montgomery, AL: Old Faithful Press, 1984) 48.

[3]Frances J. Roberts, *Come Away My Beloved* (Old Tappan, NJ: Fleming H. Revell Co., 1973) 93-94.

[4]Hannah Hurnard, *The Winged Life* (Wheaton, IL: Tyndale House Publishers, Inc., 1978) 44.

[5]Anne Morrow Lindbergh, *The Gift From the Sea* (New York: Pantheon, 1955) 23-24.

[6]Gordon MacDonald, *Ordering Your Private World* (Nashville: Oliver Nelson Publishers, 1985) 9-10.

[7]Mrs. Charles Cowman, *Springs in the Valley* (Grand Rapids: Zondervan Publishing House, 1939) 31.

Chapter 10
[1]W.J. Rolfe, ed., *The Complete Poetical Works of*

Tennyson (Boston: Houghton Mifflin Co., 1898) 101.

[2]Bishop Augustine, *Augustine Confessions: Augustine of Hippo* (Grand Rapids: Sovereign Grace Publishers, 1971) 32.

[3]Mrs. Charles Cowman, *Streams in the Desert,* vol. 1 (Grand Rapids: Zondervan Publishing House, 1925) 51.

[4]Charles R. Swindoll, *Come Before Winter* (Portland, OR: Multnomah Press, 1985) 156-57.

[5]Swindoll, *Come* 156-57.

[6]Frances J. Roberts, *Progress of Another Pilgrim* (Ojai, CA: The King's Press, 1970) 75.

[7]Larry Richards, *When It Hurts Too Much to Wait* (Waco, TX: Word Books, 1985) 45, 138.